FAMILY FINANCES
FOR THE FLABBERGASTED

FAMILY FINANCES
FOR THE FLABBERGASTED

JANENE WOLSEY BAADSGAARD

DESERET BOOK COMPANY
SALT LAKE CITY, UTAH

Library of Congress Cataloging-in-Publication Data

Baadsgaard, Janene Wolsey.
    Family finances for the flabbergasted / Janene Wolsey Baadsgaard.
      p.   cm.
    Includes bibliographical references and index.
    ISBN 0-87579-895-0
      1. Finance, Personal. 2. Work and family. 3. Home-based
businesses. 4. Home economics. 5. Finance, Personal—Religious
aspects—Christianity. I. Title.
    HG179.B23   1995
    332.024—dc20   95-2011
                                                                            CIP

Printed in the United States of America

10   9   8   7   6   5   4   3   2

For Ross,
who teaches me to balance the book of life

CONTENTS

CONTENTS

INTRODUCTION

Flabbergasted parents, as a rule, do not write or read books about family finances—we're too busy running junior to ball practice, chasing runaway shopping carts, holding down a job or two, sorting darks from lights, and figuring out 101 ways to fix frozen hamburger. If we ever get a moment of solitude, it's because we've locked ourselves in the bathroom. The last thing we want to read is some expert's advice on family finances so we can feel even more guilty than we already do.

But the problem is . . . if a flabbergasted parent never writes a financial book, all we end up with is a bunch of books by experts who can't remember what flabbergasted feels like!

I've read all the financial advice books by experts, and frankly they didn't help much. I need practical, easy-to-understand advice and some help seeing the big picture, but when I read or listen to the experts, I come away feeling totally overwhelmed by everything I don't know—and then I can't remember it when I need it anyway.

Inexpert as I have felt, everywhere I go these days some stranger pulls me aside and asks me the same question, "How do you do it with all those kids?"

People who know me phrase the question like this: "With your modest salary, how are you making ends meet?"

People who *really* know me ask, "How did you get out of debt when you make a fraction of the income we do and have three times as many kids?"

This book is my answer.

I am not, by any stretch of the imagination, a financial guru. If I hear someone talking about stock, I think they're discussing cattle. Bonds are something newborns and mothers forge on the delivery table. My offspring always ask their *father* to help them with math homework. The most profound bit of financial wisdom I've passed along to my posterity lately is the answer I gave my son the other day: "No dear, I can't keep writing checks as long as I have blank ones."

But . . . during the past twenty years, I've written literally hundreds of columns, magazine articles, and books about family issues (in the midst of giving birth to my own). I've interviewed everyone from John Bradshaw on the inner child to Erma Bombeck on where to find my sense of humor. I've learned a simple truth: Experts disagree on everything. I'm also a tightwad dropout because I'm no longer convinced that the secret to financial independence for families is reusing vacuum bags and stomping on toilet paper rolls so your kids can't unwind them so fast.

The problem is, financial experts and frugality zealots don't address the real issues about money. They believe the three major financial issues are *making* money, *saving* money, and *spending* money. Peace of mind concerning family financial matters includes those things, but it also involves a larger perspective or clearer vision. It's great to save money and it's smart to wisely invest, but sometimes it's perfectly all right to get confused and put our CDs in the stereo.

Most financial books are based on several erroneous assumptions:

1. That temporal and spiritual things are separate. (But spiritual and temporal matters are *always* connected.)

2. That money is all-important. (Contrary to popular opinion, money is *not* important. On the other hand, our feelings about money *are* important.)

3. That an understanding of money is complex and difficult. (Actually, there are only five principles that govern wise dealings

with money. Knowledge of these principles helps us make choices that bring joy and a sense of peace; ignorance brings dissatisfaction and despair.)

4. That the size of our checking account is everything. (The truth: Our attitude, or the condition of our hearts, is everything.)

None of us has a guarantee against financial difficulties. We can't control financial challenges that result from natural disasters, accidents, illness, unemployment, evil choices by others, weather, government leaders, or war. We *can* control our attitude and ability to deal with financial problems or prosperity. We *can* control our pride, debt, envy, and selfishness.

I wrote this book because I feel the experts are neglecting the really important stuff. Even though I'm a flabbergasted, nonexpert mother of eight fire-breathing children, I've learned some financial principles you don't have to have a degree to understand.

Do I have all the answers? No. Nobody does. Our teenage daughter just totaled the car, the baby's got the flu, and our income tax forms just came in the mail, but . . . if I remember and live these simple principles, I sure feel a lot better about life.

CHAPTER 1

The Best Things in Life Aren't Things

Wherefore, do not spend money for that which is of no worth, nor your labor for that which cannot satisfy.

—2 NEPHI 9:51

ENOUGH

Once there was a young girl who lived in a small house in a small town. Except for having to do the dishes, make her bed, and clean her room, the young girl had a pretty good life.

"When I grow up," the girl said to herself one day, "I will live in a large white house out in the country and I will have a small, quiet family. I will be wise, rich, and famous. I will hire a maid to cook and clean. My husband will cherish me and my children will honor me. When I am grown up enough, then I will be happy."

The girl got into her pajamas, brushed her teeth, and went to bed. Then she woke up in the morning, went to school, and soon she was grown up. After she graduated from high school, the girl dreamed of going to the university, but her parents didn't have enough money.

"There is never enough," the girl said to herself. "When I have enough money to go to the university, I will be happy."

So the girl took three jobs, one at the library, one cleaning apartments for her landlord, and one cooking at the diner. After three years of working three jobs and studying at the university, the young girl was tired and lonely.

"When I don't have to work and someone loves me enough, then I will be happy," the girl said.

Later, a young man asked the girl to marry him. She said yes, quit her three jobs and school, and went to live with the young man in a tiny apartment without windows. Soon the girl

3

was lonely again because now her husband was working three jobs and studying at the university.

"When I have enough children to keep me company, then I will be happy," the girl said.

The girl had two babies before her second wedding anniversary.

"I never have enough sleep," the girl said. "When I have enough sleep, then I will be happy."

One day the girl sat down at the kitchen table covered with spilled milk and said, "There is not enough money to finish my degree at the university. When I have enough money to finish my degree, then I will be happy."

So the girl saved her money, then went back to school to finish her degree. After many papers and late-night study sessions while rocking her fussy babies and studying for exams, the girl graduated from the university.

Then one day the girl said, "There is not enough room in this house. I have too many children and they are too noisy. When I have a large house in the country, then I will be happy."

So the girl saved her money. Then she found out she was going to have another baby. She was not expecting this news.

"I have too many babies," the girl said. "I don't have a big enough house or enough strength. I will be happy when I stop having babies."

Finally, after many years, the girl and her family bought a large house in the country.

"I don't have enough energy to keep up this large house and clean up after the children," the girl said. "When the children are raised and I can move back to a small house, then I will be happy."

The years went by, the children were growing up, and the girl was still waiting. Her husband didn't always cherish her. Sometimes he ignored her and watched basketball on the television.

"You don't give me enough attention," the girl told her husband. "You love basketball more than you love me."

"But I keep the car filled with gas and make waffles every Saturday," her husband answered.

The girl was not listening.

The girl's children didn't always honor her. Sometimes they said mean things and came home after curfew.

"You children don't obey me enough or keep your rooms clean enough," the girl said to her children.

"But we are growing up and soon we will be gone and you will miss us," the children answered.

The girl was not listening.

"I don't have enough help around the house," the girl said one day as she sorted the socks. "I still have to cook my own meals and clean my own house. My children are noisy, not quiet, and I live in a red brick house, not white."

The socks did not answer. The girl went to a therapist because she was talking to socks. The therapist told the girl that her family did not understand or appreciate her enough. The therapist said that the girl must go home and go to bed and not get out until she was appreciated and understood. The girl was glad. She did not want to get up because her family was too big and too noisy and they did not love her enough.

The girl stayed in bed for a long time. She had lots of time for thinking.

"Why didn't you make me wise or rich or famous?" the girl said to God one night. "Why didn't you give me a husband and children who would honor and cherish me? Why do I have to work so hard? Why don't I ever have enough?"

"You've always had enough," God said. "But you weren't listening."

The girl thought for a long, long while.

That night, the girl dreamed a new dream. She dreamed that what she always wanted was a red brick house, a husband who made waffles on Saturday, and many noisy children to keep her company.

The next day, the girl got out of bed. She did not go back to the therapist. The girl found her husband watching a basketball game on television. She sat on his lap and kissed him. She found her children yelling in the family room. She hugged them, one by one. Then she walked downstairs to the laundry room and talked to the dirty socks. The socks answered her because the woman was listening. 🙚

THE REAL VALUE OF MONEY

The first time I questioned the value of money was when I was a college student touring Europe with several friends on a Eurail Pass. Almost daily, my companions and I found ourselves in a new country where we had to change our money before anyone would accept it. Unfortunately, the line to exchange our currency at the train station was always about 26 million miles long. Before I got to the end of the currency exchange line, I always had to use the ladies' room. European ladies' room attendants simply would not let me use their facilities until I exchanged my money.

While I nervously stood in that long line to switch my money, I realized the paper rectangles and metal coins in my purse were a game. People take the game very seriously when they believe they understand the rules. Those ladies' room attendants, who were built like defensive linemen, by the way, wouldn't let me near the door unless I had the right *kind* of money. Even if I were the richest woman in the world at that instant, it would not even buy me the most basic of necessities.

I'd grown up valuing U.S. dollars because I understood the goods or services I could exchange for them. Every time I entered a new country, I was forced to relearn the game. It took me an additional twenty years to understand the true game and to begin to set my own rules.

Money will enable us to buy just about anything in the world. But the things we can buy with money are always of this world. Things of this world don't last. I'm an amateur archaeologist, so I know. I spent a summer digging up the ancient site of Beersheba in Israel. The site had seen several thousand years of civilization—but all we found to dig up was a few broken dishes and a rock or two from an old foundation. It doesn't matter how much we acquire; given time, all our stuff will break down and turn to dust.

On the other hand, when someone gets up on their soapbox and tells me money doesn't really matter, I usually figure they inherited their income from a wealthy deceased uncle on their father's side of the family. I'm the kind of mother who tells my children that money never grows on trees or rutabagas. I'm practical, and I often act like money *does* matter. With ten mouths to feed, I have to be practical. But, during my better moments, I understand that happiness has very little to do with money.

Just about everybody wants to be happy. But if money were the chief factor of happiness, then everybody who had money would be happy and everyone without money would be unhappy. I, for one, know several crabby rich people—who shall remain anonymous to protect *me*—and several extremely cheerful chaps who are dirt poor. So if money does not make us happy, what does?

I believe we reawaken our ability to feel joy when we change the way we *think* about money. We begin to change the way we feel about finances when we *never* allow money to make our important life decisions.

For example, I know a nice fellow who has always wanted to be a doctor. He wishes almost every day that he had gone to medical school, and he only tolerates his present work. He often tells me he would have made a great doctor because he is not only intelligent but is compassionate as well. I think he's right. Even though being a doctor was always his dream, however, he never applied to attend medical school. He didn't believe he had enough money.

I also know a woman who *did* go to medical school. This friend of mine now owns a medical practice in a major city. When this woman was growing up, she noticed that all the doctors in her small town had the biggest houses and drove the most expensive cars. She made the decision to become a doctor because of money. She didn't consider the difficulties involved.

Both of my friends are unhappy today. They let money rule their decisions, and, in the end, made what was for them the wrong choice.

Most of us, whether we earn a little or a lot, allow money to make far too many of our important decisions. We allow it to limit our hopes and dreams and determine our life choices. Money simply doesn't deserve all this respect—it's not an accurate yardstick or compass. We are the masters of our choices. It's important that we not give money the power to distort our perceptions of life and what would truly make us happy.

I remember a day not too long ago when I was having another "poor me" attack. I was contemplating how much happier I'd be if I lived in a beautiful new home staffed with a housekeeper, cook, nanny, and gardener. I was tired of having to clean my own house, shop, cook and clean up after every meal, take care of the children all day without help, and work in my yard every night.

One evening while I was pulling weeds in our backyard garden, my neighbor's young daughter ran over and invited me to come take a look at their pig, Penny, who had just given birth to a new batch of piglets. I put down my hoe and went over to take a look. (Or should I say, I went over to take a smell?) There sat my neighbor's immense pig hogging down her supper.

"Where are her babies?" I questioned the young girl.

"Oh, Penny rolls over on her babies and accidentally kills them, so we have to take care of them until we sell them to the Polynesians for their luaus," my little neighbor replied matter-of-factly.

Penny was certainly wallowing in the lap of luxury. She had a nice new pen to live in and food someone else provided—she didn't have to shop, cook, or clean up after herself. She had even developed an ingenious plot so someone else would have to take care of her children. She never had to work or worry. All she had to do was wallow. Penny didn't have to worry about income taxes, car insurance rates for adolescents, flossing her teeth, or what to fix for supper. All she had to do was lounge around all day and eat.

While I was peeking through the slat into that pig's pen, it occurred to me that Penny's life consisted of everything I had been longing for. Yet for some reason, at that moment I wasn't quite ready to trade her places. I had a strange feeling that if my life were suddenly free from work, children, worry, mealtime hassles, and heartache, it might not be quite so interesting.

I'm convinced that the happiest people are those who have the most interesting thoughts. To have interesting thoughts, we need to free our minds from a preoccupation with unimportant things— including the making and spending of material wealth.

The happiest among us are those who spend a lifetime culti-vating their minds—selecting the seeds of positive thoughts and weeding out the negative. (Remember: "As [a man] thinketh . . . so is he." [Prov. 23:7.]) My family and I live out in the country on a few acres of ground. The first year we lived there, we watered our ground from sprinklers, diligently producing acres of weeds as well as fruits and vegetables. The next year we tried a drip system, where our garden and mini-orchard were watered from a setup that released water slowly at specific places along the hose. Without water, the unwanted weeds soon withered and died; meanwhile, the fruits and vegetables, which got the water, thrived.

Our minds, like a garden, need careful nurturing. We can't always choose the weeds or thoughts that drift into our minds, but we can choose what to water and what to neglect. Every good or bad seed that is allowed to grow in our minds will take root and blossom into action. Our life's harvest is gleaned from what was first a tiny thought.

We can choose to focus on what we have instead of what we don't have. We can choose to let feelings of gratitude color the way we see the world. We can choose to become "inverse paranoids" (some people would call these "optimists"), believing that all circumstances and events and relationships in our lives will work out for the best if we are searching for the good. We can choose to be happy.

We can choose to love and be loved. Love will never fail us as long as we give it, and when we see loving relationships rather than expensive things as the measure of success, we will make the choices, daily, that draw us closer to those we care about.

"Where your treasure is, there will your heart be also." (Matt. 6:21.) Children are smart. Children instinctively understand that we give our time to what we love most. If parents spend most of their time making or spending money, children quickly learn what comes first in their parents' hearts. Why are we so slow to catch on to what really counts?

It's easy to confuse self-worth with net worth and believe money can solve our problems. Money never solved anybody's problems. If I inherited a million dollars tomorrow, I'd still have all of my old problems, plus a few new ones to boot. Money does not solve problems. People solve problems. Money can't think. People think.

Another reason we've allowed money to influence the way we perceive ourselves and others is that we believe money will give us what we lack, and we all feel lacking in some way. For instance, if we lack respect from those around us, we think people will give us more respect if we have more money. In fact, the people who give more respect to those who have money are called snobs. Snobs don't make good friends and are incapable of offering true respect.

If we search for wealth in the wrong places, it's like running a lifelong race with no finish line. Who wants to run that kind of race?

We depose money as king when we reenthrone time as the ultimate measure of prosperity. We've all been given an equal inheritance of twenty-four hours a day. How we spend our time, not our money, will ultimately determine the value of our lives.

THE BEST INVESTMENT

The mental focus and energy we give to money can be a cause of mental, physical, and spiritual illness. When we think clearly about money, we become wise enough to spend our time thinking about other things that are more important, and in the end we become rich in ways that transcend money.

Everywhere we look today (and if you're not looking, don't worry, because they'll still find you), someone is giving another seminar, conference, or class on becoming more wealthy, more organized, or more beautiful, so we can buy more things or be more things. What we *really* need is a mandatory class on how to do less with more love. One of the most difficult challenges of life is wisely deciding which good activities to hold on to and which ones to let go.

Many of the most rewarding life choices can be found in our own backyards and come as we learn to do less with more relish. This occurs as we create lives that revolve around those we love, filled with feelings of gratitude instead of a desire to accumulate possessions and win the approval of others. When we gain an insight into what really matters and quit chasing a future that never exists, we begin to understand wealth and free ourselves from much ado about nothing.

Most of us already have much more than we really need. As I've traveled about the world and observed and researched other cultures, I've discovered that people don't need much in the way of possessions to be happy. Our present money-worshipping culture seems awfully soiled when compared with the majority of humble people who have populated or now populate this planet. Millions live rich, full lives in circumstances we would consider abject poverty.

It helps me keep things in perspective when I remind myself that the best things in life are free—or at least a great bargain at today's prices. For instance, I can read the same wonderful books as the wealthiest people in the world just by visiting the local library.

I can easily learn about exotic foreign lands by viewing a public television program. I sleep in a comfortable bed every night and enjoy the miracle of a warm shower every morning.

I can enjoy fresh food year round. When my clothes get dirty, I can throw them into a couple of automatic machines and get clean, dry clothes back. For pennies a day, I can read about all the important news of the entire world just by picking up a newspaper. A school bus picks up my children for educational opportunities every morning and drops them off every afternoon.

When I want to exercise, all I need is a pair of shoes, a little enthusiasm, and two feet. While I'm out there walking on the country roads around my house, I can enjoy a magnificent sunset for no charge whatsoever and find immense satisfaction observing a farmer's field of wheat rippling in the breeze.

Someone once said that life may be expensive, but it includes free trips around the sun. How we feel about our lives is usually all a matter of attitude, including our ability to feel thankful for simple things. It takes effort and focus, but we can all develop a broader perspective that allows us to view things as they really are. Things as they really are can be downright amazing. Money can buy us a house, but not a home. Money can buy medicine, but it may not buy us health. Money can buy us amusement, but not necessarily happiness. We don't need more money to be prosperous. We need only dream, like the girl in the story, that what we always wished for is what we already have.

One night when I was a young child, I sat on the back-door step with my father. The stars in the night sky were especially bright that evening. Suddenly from the corner of my eye, I saw a shooting star.

"Dad!" I said. "Did you see that?"

My father nodded.

"I've heard that if you see a shooting star, you can make a wish and it will come true."

Dad put his arm around me.

"Want to know how to really make wishes come true?" Dad asked.

"Sure."

"See all those other stars? Every night, the sky is filled with them and we hardly notice because there are so many and they shine every night without fail. If those stars made a once a year performance, all the people on this planet would wait and watch with excitement and wonder. [My father was a great fan of Emerson.] But because the stars shine for us every night, we forget to look up. We forget to notice. Jan, if you can look up each night and see those heavenly lights with the same awe and appreciation you just gave that one lone shooting star, your dreams will come true."

FAMILIES FIRST

One of the easiest ways to lose sight of the big picture is to forget that our families should come first—before commitments to work, community, church, recreation, or anything else. Family life is tough. Let me tell you, it's much easier to become a workaholic, churchaholic, projectaholic, or playaholic than a loving, nurturing mother or father. It's also easy to take our families for granted.

The other night, my husband took all the children to the store without me. I was so excited to have a little peace, I literally clicked my heels in the upstairs hallway when I heard the loaded car drive away.

I walked through the entire house without one person yelling, "It's not fair!"

No one needed help with homework, love life, buttons, or shoes. Nobody needed a ride to work, church, a friend's house, or basketball practice. I read the entire newspaper without one interruption.

Snuggling back into the soft folds of the overstuffed recliner, I sighed, "Is this the life or what!"

An hour or so went by and my family didn't reappear. Another hour went by and I found myself pacing in the hallway wondering if they'd been in an accident. I started wiping down countertops and refrigerator doors. I straightened pillows and picture frames. I dusted the top of the piano. I never dust the top of the piano.

I was getting desperate. Before I knew what had come over me, I found myself pressing my nose against the west window, anxiously watching for car lights.

When I heard the station wagon pull back into the driveway, and heard the sounds of several car doors slamming, kids yelling— and glass breaking—I took a deep breath and sighed once more. With those wonderful familiar sounds, I knew I was now in for several hours of chaos, baths, stories, and homework coaching. Strange thing was, at that moment, I couldn't wait to get started.

The rigors of family life are private lessons that teach us how to live in and relish the present. We can't go back or forward in time, and it's foolish to wish the present away. So, lately, I've decided to work on truly important things, like my ability to watch the kids track mud in the house without going into cardiac arrest. I've decided to eat dessert first and find time—every day—to sing a little, play a little, work a little, think a little, and pray a little.

I'm going to remember to catch more sunrises and moonrises. I'm going to hug my family, friends, and even strangers more often. I have plans to smile more and go barefoot in the grass. I've made a note in my weekly planner to be silly and remember to laugh at myself—especially when I think I have all the answers. I've decided to be more gentle with myself and the other guy—especially after I've made a mistake.

You see, I honestly believe that we don't need to do more or have more. Life comes with an expiration date. We don't know when ours will come due. Because our time is a limited resource, it is the most precious thing we possess. The choices we make about how to balance our lives or spend our time will always be difficult, but if we are wise, we will understand that a lifestyle is not a life.

For example, there are hundreds of voices out there today telling married couples to delay or avoid parenthood. It seems to make perfect sense to give education, cars, homes, careers, privacy, and freedom a higher place on our list of priorities. My husband and I made the decision to have our children while we were young, dumb, and penniless, and I'm sure glad we did.

If my husband and I had waited until we could afford to have children, we would have never had any. We didn't have children because of our income. We had children on faith. It's amazing how motivated and creative we became to stretch those precious dollars when we looked down into our newborns' eyes. Money can't buy love. A baby who is loved will not care if he sleeps in the bottom drawer of his parents' dresser or in a lavishly decorated nursery.

If we wait until we have all the education we desire before we have children, that education will not mean as much to us. My husband had to work several jobs while he was a full-time student to support his growing family. When he graduated, he had a diploma, a great deal of practical work experience, and two daughters. My education was delayed for a few years when I made the choice to become a mother. Later, when I went back to school, I had matured and knew what I wanted to study. I was so hungry for knowledge and felt so privileged to be in the classroom again, I was a much better student. When I graduated with honors, six of my children were there to share the joy.

If we wait to buy a car or a house before we have children, we will be in for a major disappointment. Once our material goal is accomplished, it will never be enough. We will wake up the next day and still be the same old unsatisfied selves. By contrast, when we do kind things for other people, it changes our hearts. It is difficult to change our hearts, but when we do we are able to recognize and savor the simple things that bring lasting joy. Children offer us the ultimate opportunity for a change of heart.

If we wait until we are established in our careers before we have children, we may miss the boat. A career is not a life. A career is something we do to sustain life. A meaningful life includes people, many people, especially children. Women who are blessed with the capacity to bear children have only a few years to use that gift. There will always be someone who can replace us in our careers. The only place where we are absolutely essential and irreplaceable is in the lives of our family.

If we don't want to give up our freedom by having children, we may find that we are trapped in our own selfishness. In the twenty-four-hour-a-day job of rearing children, we discover that we must daily give and give and give to cope with the demands children bring. Children will free us from our selfishness if we let them. We discover ourselves when we lose ourselves and that is what true freedom is all about.

If we don't have children because we don't want to give up our privacy, we may find ourselves alone when we don't want to be. Sometimes we have to give up the things we think we want in order to obtain the things we truly need. There will be many times in our lives when we will not want to be alone. There will be important times when we are sick or dying or even extremely happy. Sharing these times with someone we love and someone who loves us helps to make life worth living. Creating a family has the potential to fill our lives with the greatest challenges and joys life has to offer.

I like to flip through the newspaper in the evening and cut out coupons. I have only one minor problem. Most of the time when I hand the coupon to the cashier, she hands it back and says, "I'm sorry but your coupon has expired."

I peer down at the worthless wrinkled paper in my hands, squint at the fine print, look dumb, and say something like, "Why, what do you know . . . you're right. I forgot to notice. Sorry about that."

I often make the same mistake with my children. It's really unfortunate our children aren't born with a series of manufacturers' coupons attached to their belly buttons. Sometimes we parents need expiration dates to help us appreciate childhood before time runs out.

When my oldest boy used to wave at me from the school bus

while I stood at the front-room window in my pajamas, I didn't think anything of it. Then one day this son, who had recently started junior high and was actually taking baths without being bribed, asked me not to wave at him anymore, especially in my pajamas, and if I had to kiss him, would I please wait until no one was looking.

Now, when my younger eight- and nine-year-old boys jump on bus 89E for Larsen Elementary School and blow me armfuls of kisses, I notice. I know it won't last. I have learned you have to cash in valuable things while you still have the chance.

I used to droop into the baby's bedroom with bloodshot eyes and pick up my newborn baby like a robot. . . . Plug bottle in head end. Secure wet wipes. Clean bottom end.

Now I steal into the nursery late at night and stand at baby Ashley's crib for a long while, looking down at my daughter's full, soft face in the white blankets. My baby has been transforming herself into a little girl lately . . . overnight. Her legs and arms are spilling out the spokes of the tiny bed. Soon I'll be taking down her crib and storing it in the garage along with the stroller, car seat, high chair, and pink plastic bathtub. My daughter will outgrow babyhood and I want to be there when she does. I want to notice before the coupon expires.

If someone would just tell us, warn us, that childhood is a gift— a fragile gift. Like a leaf in the wind, our children are here one minute, then are gone on the next breeze. There should be an official notice posted, an international warning issued for parents. We need to read the fine print before we get up to the cashier and realize we're too late.

Notice to Parent: We will redeem this coupon for the face value of one child plus 8 cents handling if submitted in compliance with the childhood redemption policy, incorporated herein by reference. Void if reproduced or where prohibited by law. Cash value 1/20 cent. Mail to: Childhood Appreciation Corporation. Dept. #30049, Last Chance Drive, Home 84660. (LIMIT ONE COUPON PER CHILD.)

When we come to the end of our lives, we may not regret the money we didn't earn, the degrees we didn't hang on the wall, or the honors we didn't obtain. We *will* regret the time we didn't spend with our spouses, our children, our parents, or our friends. Time and money are a finite commodity at every house. We can spend our time and money on things that will wear out, or we can invest them in people. I presently hold stock in ten great commodities named Ross, Janene, April, Aubrey, Jordan, Arianne, Joseph, Jacob, Amy, and Ashley.

Fifty years from now it won't matter at all what kind of car I drove, or what kind of house I lived in. It won't matter how much money I had in the bank or what kind of clothes I wore. Fifty years from now, my life will have meaning only if I've taken the time to be a positive influence in the life of a child. In a very real sense, children are the only way we can send a message to tomorrow, the surest way to give our lives meaning.

Perhaps the most pressing reason to give our families top priority is that our time together is limited. Husbands and wives die . . . children grow up . . . nothing remains the same.

I had to put my daughter April on an airplane to Japan a while back. When they started announcing boarding rules over the loud speaker, April and I gave each other a nervous smile, then wrapped our arms around each other. Then she walked through the entrance and disappeared. Just like that.

All the years of late-night feedings, bronchitis, recitals, powder-puff football games, proms, driver's license tests, and car accidents flashed before me. It was something like they say happens just before you die, only it was April's life I saw, not mine. The problem was, I had to stay alive, walk back to the parking lot, and leave without her.

It was so awful and so wonderful all wrapped up together that I didn't know how to feel. In what seemed to be only a few short moments, I'd gone from giving birth to giving wings. Nobody warned me it would feel so good and hurt so much.

As my children have begun their flight, I've found myself reevaluating the short time I have to spend with my sons and daughters before they leave home. Even though I realize I know my children, I sometimes look into their eyes and wonder if I truly understand them. Those we should know the best often remain the greatest mystery, because we've seen and loved each other as so many different people through the years.

What most children don't understand is that their parents see them through "time-warp" eyes. We don't see *only* a talented, confident young woman or man getting ready to graduate from high school or get married. We *also* see a premature infant struggling for her first breath, a four-year-old with her finger up her nose during the entire Mother's Day program, a six-year-old missing two front teeth, a bloody eight-year-old after his bicycle accident, a dejected fourteen-year-old after his first junior high dance, and a sixteen-year-old leaving on her first date.

What many children may not understand is that their middle-aged mother or father (in orthopedic shoes and having a bad hair day) was once a scared twenty-two-year-old fumbling with the diaper pins, an embarrassed twenty-six-year-old crying through the Mother's Day program, a frightened twenty-eight-year-old passing out in the hall after the accident, a proud thirty-year-old flashing pictures at the Christmas play, an understanding thirty-four-year-old trying to share an awful first junior high dance disaster, and a confused thirty-six-year-old with her nose pressed against the living room window as her daughter drives away with her first young man.

Children and parents grow up together, and it's hard sometimes. We affect each other's lives more than anyone else. We're both struggling to sort out life in each other's presence. We live in the same rooms and eat the same food, yet sometimes we remain strangers to each other's hearts. It's difficult for us to impress each other because we've seen each other when we wake up in the morning, yet we can impress each other the most with a certain wink of the eye or gentle touch of a hand.

Children know their parents' occupations, dispositions, and actions, but they seldom know their mother's or father's secret dreams or fears. There are no experts in family making, only amateurs. As we fumble about trying to fill each other's needs, we frequently end up stepping on each other's toes. We often lose precious time longing for something from each other that was there all along. There is not enough time to postpone forgiving. Parents spend a lifetime creating a home that children must leave. It hurts on both ends to learn the difficult art of roots and wings.

With all the holding on and letting go, I hope I'll be able to put my false teeth in when I'm ninety-six and say, "I didn't miss a doggone thing."

MARRIAGE MATTERS

It's also easy to let our commitments to our children take priority over the most important relationship, our marriage. It's easy to lose focus, forget the big picture, and slowly let romance and magic fade. I remember a time when I realized the greatest gift I could give my children was to love their father.

I was driving our gang of children back from a trip to the library when I heard the words of a popular country song on the radio.

" . . . Can I have this dance for the rest of my life?" the country singer crooned.

Even though I am the harried mother of eight (and was driving a saggy-rear-end station wagon), romantic words and a catchy tune still give me goose bumps. As I listened to that song, I remembered all the dances my husband and I had attended before we married and how it felt to be in his arms with soft lights, a live band, and the feeling I was twirling about two feet off the dance floor.

"I can't remember the last time Ross asked me to dance," I thought as I rounded the corner for home. "Ten, maybe fifteen years."

The music faded. The noise in my car did not. The children

were throwing words and apple-core bombs over my head, but I was too exhausted to get mad. I drove in the driveway, parked the car, and herded the kids into the house.

Later, I found myself humming the words of that song at the oddest times—like when I was scrubbing the frying pan, bathing the baby, or sorting laundry. I even danced with a dirty red flannel shirt once in the laundry room when no one was looking. (I often have visions that I'll drop dead under a stack of dirty laundry and no one will notice until they run out of clean socks.)

Then, a few days later, I was running around like a chicken with my head cut off trying to get the children ready for church. I was racing the clock to: get myself dressed, fix a meal, clean up the atomic-food-bomb blast after the children finished, curl and comb several heads of hair, locate several matching shoes, assemble toddler quiet books, fill the nursery bucket, help a son with a Primary talk, find a replacement for the pianist and chorister, "guilt" a child into wearing a tie, change a diaper, help my daughter decorate her secret-sister basket, and find time to take an aspirin.

I must have looked alarmingly hassled when I dashed down-stairs to the laundry room holding the baby on one hip and drag-ging a toddler with one leg—while several other children demanded my immediate attention to help them with their hair, necktie, or shoelaces. Meanwhile, my husband was relaxing in the rocking chair listening to music, and the only thing he was holding was the paper.

I gave him *THE LOOK,* then proceeded to rummage through the clean clothes in the laundry room. Suddenly and unexpectedly, I felt a tap on my shoulder.

"May I have this dance?" Ross asked.

My mouth dropped.

Without waiting for an answer, he swept me out of the laundry room and into the family room, where he proceeded to waltz me around the sofa and over several children wrestling on the floor. Because Ross is more than a foot taller than I am, I have to dance on my tiptoes. Dancing tiptoed tends to make me a little light-headed.

Just as everything became a blur in the swirling room, every-thing else came into focus. As my husband drew me closer, I knew that dirty laundry and Sunday shoes were unimportant details—details that were distracting me from more important business.

My daughter went to church without her hair curled that Sunday and my son wore his holey socks and no tie because I had more important things to do—like waltz around the family room on my tiptoes with my husband . . . one more time.

OUR OTHER FAMILY

An equally important part of spending our time wisely by putting people first is remembering that we are all brothers and sis-ters. We are all family and connected in ways we can't see.

One summer, on a hot July holiday weekend, my husband and I decided to take our family on a hike to the top of the mountain framed in our living room window. We wanted the children to feel the sense of accomplishment that comes at the completion of some-thing difficult. We wanted the children to look up at Maple Mountain and remember how their perspective changed when they were able to see things in a new way.

We started the long hike singing songs, joking, sharing water and candy, but as the hours ticked by and the sun rose higher and hotter into the sky, the happy conversations retreated into huffing and puffing, moaning and groaning.

It was a long, difficult hike with new vistas opening at each hill-top. We threaded our way through open meadows filled with wild-flowers as tall as our heads and secluded aspen- and pine-canopied trails. Right before we reached the mountain ridge, we had to climb a steep, rocky slope in the glaring midday sun.

After one particularly painful fall, my young son yelled out, "Why did we have to come on this stupid hike anyway? I'm hungry. I'm tired. I have to go to the bathroom."

Without a word, my husband put our son on his back and started back up the cliff. The rest of us locked arms, forming a human chain up the steep, rocky incline. Long after we all thought we would like to die and end our misery, we reached the first ridge, our bodies dripping with sweat, smelling bad, and looking worse.

Once on top, the pine-scented wind washed over us and took our breath away. There before us, like some giant patchwork quilt, lay farmers' fields in various shades of green and gold, seamed together with long stretches of gray road. Utah Lake shimmered in the distance. Hawks circled below. Cities and towns nestled in groves of trees along the oak-covered foothills.

The children were perfectly quiet. It was the first time they'd seen their valley from this lofty perspective.

"I didn't know everything fit together like that," my daughter said. "When I'm down there in it, I can't see it."

We are all family. Limited vision down in the valley causes us to believe that we are separate beings—that our lives are not connected. In reality, we are all brothers and sisters. Like pieces of a quilt, the fabric of our lives touches others in ways we will never know. Everything fits together like that. It does. It always will.

The human family marks important dates of arrival and departure. Whether we welcome a new child into life's circle through the miracle of birth, release a grown child from the nest for college or marriage, or remember a missing place at the table—families bind the world together as they gather to honor life's renewal and the passing of time.

From the day that first granddaughter is held high in the air for all the family to see and coo over, to the day we send grandfather back home to God, we need to remember that brothers and sisters, fathers and mothers, sons and daughters are more than we suppose. Life draws us too far apart for us not to savor the times we have together.

A young couple we know lost their three-year-old son in a car accident. When I went to the mortuary and saw our friends, still bruised and bandaged from the accident, sitting next to their son's small casket, I realized that all of us are only a moment away from unanticipated endings. At any moment, everything we take for granted, including our health and our family, can be taken away.

It is largely with our families that we invest our dreams and hopes. It is with these precious few we play out our lives. There is no one else on this planet with whom we have more in common. Our families can't be replaced. Who will care when we are gone? Who will hold us in their arms when we die? Who will miss our companionship, the way we laugh, our gentle hands or warm embrace? The family we have loved, and who will have loved us, will help form the sum of our lives.

My baby daughter recently discovered the game of holding on and letting go. She concentrates so intently her tongue sticks out when she picks up a single small Cheerio. Then without a thought she opens her pinched fingers, dropping the cereal to the floor. When she realizes the Cheerio won't come back, she cries.

I'm not so different. I still play at holding on and letting go. I realize nothing will bring time back, not ever, not even for a moment. Life is short—too short—to leave the loving undone, the appreciation unfelt, the joy unembraced.

The best things in life aren't things. The only power money has over our lives is the power we give it to control our thoughts and our time. Time, that great equalizer and our divine inheritance, makes putting people first absolutely vital to our peace of mind and our ability to feel joy.

There is honor and a deep sustaining joy that comes with creating a family and helping each individual in the circle reach his or her potential. Developing a truly loving relationship with our parents, siblings, spouses, and each of our children is perhaps the greatest achievement in life.

CHAPTER 2

Managing Our Money Before It Manages Us

Pay the debt. . . . Release thyself from bondage.

—D&C 19:35

FREE

Once there was a little boy who was happy and free. The boy heard his mother singing when she pushed him in the swing and it made him feel happy. He heard the birds singing in the trees and it made him happy.

"I want to be a fine musician when I grow up," the boy told his piano teacher. "I want to make people happy."

The boy's teacher smiled. "You can be a fine musician," she said. "If you give me seven years, I will make you a fine musician."

The boy believed the teacher, so he gave her seven years. Each day, the boy practiced the piano until his head ached. But he did not stop.

After seven years the boy was a fine musician, but he had no money.

"I want to have some money," the boy told his father.

The boy's father smiled. "You can have money," he said. "If you go to the university for many years and get a good job, then you can have some money."

The boy believed his father, so he went to the university for many years. When he had his degree, the boy got a job at a computer software company and worked in the research and development department. After many years the boy was promoted, but the boy had no family.

"I want a family," the boy told his mother.

The boy's mother smiled. "You can have a family," she

27

said. "If you marry a woman and have children, you can have a family."

The boy believed his mother. The boy married a woman and had children. Many years later the boy had a family, but he did not have a big house or a new car.

"I want a big house," the boy told his banker.

The boy's banker smiled. "You can have a big house and a new car," he said. "If you give me thirty years, you can have a big house."

"I want a new car," the boy told the car salesman.

The car salesman smiled. "You can have a new car, if you give me four years," he said.

The boy believed the banker and the car salesman, and he gave them thirty-four years. Each day he went to work at the computer software company in the morning and came home tired late at night.

"I need to get away from my life," the boy told the travel agent. "I want to travel to Europe."

The travel agent smiled. "You can travel to Europe if you give me money," she said.

"But I am out of money," the boy said.

"Then you will have to speak to your banker," the travel agent said.

"I want new clothes," the boy's wife said. "And I need my own car to go shopping."

"I will have to speak to my banker," the boy said.

"We want new toys," the boy's children said.

"I will have to speak to my banker," the boy said.

So the boy went to speak to his banker. His banker did not smile.

"You have no more years to sell," the boy's banker said. "Get to work. You have thirty-four years to go."

The boy believed his banker. He went home and sat down on the sofa.

"I want my life back," the boy said to himself one night with his lap full of bills. "Where is the music I used to hear?"

The boy went into his bedroom and closed the door.

"I want to be free," the boy said to God. "I want to be a good man, but I am trapped."

"You are a good man," God said. "If you give me the rest of your life, you can be free."

The boy believed God.

So the boy traded his large new home for a small cozy one, sold his new car for a used one, and paid off all his bills. Then the boy started a dance band with his co-workers at the computer company during their lunch break. Instead of traveling to Europe, the boy stepped into his backyard and discovered his wife and children. He heard the birds singing in the trees and it made him happy. The boy sang for his children while he pushed them in the swings.

The boy's children smiled.

Sometimes late at night after the children had gone to bed, the boy took his wife into the living room, where he played love songs for her on the piano.

The boy's wife smiled.

"I have my life back," the boy said.

Then the boy smiled. ✍

GETTING CONTROL OF YOUR MONEY

When I wake up on Saturday morning, I often decide I won't bother with my hair or makeup because it takes too much time—and all I plan to do is work in the yard or house anyway. Later in the day, if my husband invites me out to lunch or my children want me to take them shopping, I'm too uncomfortable with my appearance to go. I felt great just working around the house, but I fear I look too sloppy to be seen in public.

When I don't take the time at the beginning of the day to take care of how I look, I end up spending the rest of the day making decisions that show a preoccupation with how I look.

On the other hand, if I take a few minutes to shower, style my hair, put on a touch of makeup, and feel good about the way I look, I am free to forget my appearance. That makes me free to do lots of other things—like accept that spontaneous invitation to lunch or go on that shopping trip.

It works much the same way with our money or resources. You can fully understand that money is not the most valuable thing in your life and decide not to worry about it. But later in the day of your life, you end up making decisions or declining opportunities because you have not taken the time to manage your money wisely enough.

In the beginning, taking the time to make plans and manage your finances seems like a preoccupation with money. In the end, money management plans allow you to free up your mind and heart and get on with more important things.

Even if you realize your best investments have nothing to do with money, what do you do when the kids get hungry, cold, or tired? We all require basic necessities to survive, and one of the central purposes of money is to provide us with the resources for living. Needing money for resources to survive doesn't get you into trouble; but a preoccupation with money and resources *can*. You can be just as preoccupied with money or resources when you have too little as when you have too much. The challenge is to effectively manage your money so you can afford to forget about it.

Most of us are required to work for the necessities of life. At some point we have to put down our good intentions and take out the shovel. But too many of us put down our good intentions and take out a home equity loan instead.

Money can be your servant or your master—and it makes a lot more sense to force it to be a servant. To be master over your money, you have to be master over yourself. Money mastery is really self-mastery. Self-mastery is self-discipline, or your ability to control the thoughts that lead to your actions.

Debt, for instance, is really our unwillingness to discipline ourselves and wait. There's no pussyfooting around it—waiting is hard. Everybody hates to wait. Waiting is boring. Waiting is slow. So we rush out and buy more and get more, thinking we're having a great time—until one day we take a look at our home mortgage repayment schedule . . . and scream.

Debt is bondage. Paying off a loan is hard. Paying off a big loan is waiting, big time. Everybody hates to pay back borrowed money. Collection agencies are boring.

So there's waiting and boring stuff on both ends. We all have to get used to waiting and being bored. That's life and it's good for us, just as our mothers said.

My husband, Ross, is a banker. He makes agriculture loans to a wide assortment of farmers and ranchers. Over the years, these borrowers have taught him the secret to weathering the ups and downs of the hard economic realities of farm life. Their favorite saying is, "Thems that understands interest, collects it. Thems that *doesn't* understand interest, pays it."

A banker is a firsthand witness to the hard realities of interest payments and the really rotten stuff that comes from borrowing more money than one can reasonably expect to pay back.

If you want the freedom that comes from debt-free living, you have to be debt free. If you want to be debt free, you have to pay off all your bills. Problem is, becoming debt free is like trying to lose weight. There are a zillion plans, books, tapes, and workshops out there that promise quick results. So we pay our money and try the diet for a while, but in the end we find we're out the money and still fat. Well, there are a zillion plans, books, tapes, and workshops out there that promise financial freedom. So we pay our money, try for a while, and in the end we're out the money and still in debt.

You don't have to pay some expert to find a new, improved, faster, less painful way to pay off all your bills. There is only one way to pay off your bills: simply do it. Of course, you have to *want* to do it. Wanting to do it is the hard part, because you have to want to pay off your bills *more* than you want a new car, bigger house, new dress, or a trip to Kalamazoo. The plan you use to pay off your bills isn't as important as the wanting. After you get the wanting down, you can wax creative and figure out a way.

You can't just wake up in the morning with a zero-interest-payment certificate presented to you from the tooth fairy. You have to have a plan. When we go on a family vacation we don't just hit the road and hope for the best. Before we leave, we discuss what we want to do and make decisions. If we don't want to get lost, we generally use a map or locate checkpoint stations along the way.

Working toward debt-free living works in much the same way. If you don't have a destination in mind, discuss your plans, and use a map, you'll probably get lost.

Or if you try to live beyond your means without paying the price, you may end up like Oliver Martin. This homeless man got the shock of his life when he became a stowaway in the bathroom on a Greyhound bus.

According to the Associated Press story, some fellow passenger found Oliver and shouted, "There's a bum in the bathroom!"

By the time the passenger's shout from the back of the bus had been repeated down the aisle and reached the front, it sounded to the driver like, "There's a bomb in the bathroom!"

The bus driver slammed on the brakes as frantic passengers scrambled for the door and someone flagged down a state trooper for help. Before the mix-up was resolved, the police had closed the highway for about two hours, summoned a bomb-sniffing dog, and herded all the passengers down the highway for a quarter mile.

Poor old Oliver. He had enough for bus fare in his pocket, but he wanted to go for a ride without paying for it. Didn't work for Oliver. Won't work for us.

Lack of funds is seldom the reason most families are strapped with serious money problems.

If you want to get where you're going, in a financial sense, you have to choose your destination and be willing to pay the price to get there. The road will probably be full of potholes and twists of fate, but you'll still get there if you stay on the right road long enough.

FINANCIAL PLANNING

After you know where you're going and you're willing to pay the price, what next?

You start where you are. Every family has its own set of financial goals. For some, financial freedom means owning a home free and clear, $50,000 in the bank, and a secure retirement or low-risk investment plan in the works. For others, financial freedom means renting a home, time to develop personal talents, and the ambition and health to work at what they love right until the day they die.

No matter what the plan, it's important to remember that there is no financial freedom if there is debt. Debt-free living is the most important part of any financial plan, because there is no room to move when you are strapped to interest payments. Debt is a first-class mental distraction. But if you figure you have to be debt free by next Thursday, you'll probably give up too soon and go off the diet.

A few years back my husband and I decided that we wanted to be debt free. We defined debt free as zero interest payments. To get started, we made a list of intermediate destinations or checkpoint stations along the way to evaluate our progress. In a like manner, it's helpful for every family to choose its own destination and checkpoint stations. Our plan worked like this:

Checkpoint station #1 consisted of three things. First, we mutually committed to live on less than we earned. Second, we developed a detailed savings program. Third, we came up with a detailed debt-elimination plan.

Our debt-elimination plan was simple. We budgeted a certain amount of money for paying our debts, and we agreed not to use that money for any other purpose. We then committed to focus on paying off our smallest debt first. When that debt was paid off, we applied that entire payment amount to the next largest debt, and so on.

Checkpoint station #2 included the continuation of a controlled budget and the accumulation of a predetermined amount of savings, along with retirement reserves. At this point, our goal was to pay off all debt except the home mortgage.

Checkpoint station #3 continued the controlled budget and the savings/retirement plan. This check station also included total debt elimination, including the home mortgage.

Checkpoint station #4 includes the continuation of a controlled budget, with no new debt, and with an acceleration of our savings and retirement plan.

Even with the best of plans, events outside of your control (such as natural disasters, health problems, or bank failures), can throw you back to step one. There is no such thing as complete and final financial security in life, so it pays to rely on things you can control—such as yourself. When you learn to control your money, you develop such character traits as industry, thrift, creativity, and resourcefulness. Changed character will last. Your character is you. You, yourself, are the only thing you will never leave or lose.

I make it all sound so simple, but in reality I understand that financing a family is difficult. The demands on our financial, emotional, and spiritual reserves are never ending. It's not easy to have a controlled budget when our children put unplanned demands on our resources. Just about all parents find themselves saying things like:

"If you're cold, put on a coat. If you're hot, take off your clothes. This family will live one day of the year without using the furnace or the air conditioner even if it kills us!"

"I don't care if all the other parents pay their children cash for good grades. In this family, we excel for personal reasons."

"Why do I have to drive you to track practice so you can run circles around the field? Why don't you run to the high school, wave at the track coach, then run home? It will save me two trips."

"Why does your allowance always have to burn a hole in your pocket?"

"I just spent $287.56 on groceries. I do not want to hear one more person say that we never have anything good to eat in this house."

Families sometimes seem like bottomless pits. Raising a family creates parents who feel like the little Dutch boy, desperately trying to plug up the hole in the dike with his finger only to find the dike has sprung another leak. Too soon, you run out of fingers and toes.

How do you slow the flood and plug the money leak? You do it by reducing your expenses and by making the most of the money you already have. Every dollar you *don't* spend is worth a dollar or more in new income that you don't have to go out and earn.

TWO PRINCIPLES THAT NEVER CHANGE

There are two simple, comprehensive financial principles that never change or go out of fashion. If you want to become financially stable:

1. Spend less than you earn.
2. Don't lose what you save.

Let me explain.

1. Spend Less Than You Earn

It is not possible to be financially free unless you live on less than you earn. But the problem is, *not* spending money is right up there with broccoli and flossing, which most of us truly hate. A while back I was sitting at the dining room table with my brother-in-law, who happens to be a dentist. When you eat with dentists, the conversation invariably turns to flossing.

One of my children turned to Rick and abruptly said, "You know, Uncle Richard, I think flossing is a big pain in the neck."

Richard cleared his throat, looked my son straight in the eye, and very seriously said, "If flossing is a pain in the neck, you must not be doing it correctly."

If spending less than you earn is a pain, you're not doing it correctly. Living on less than you earn can be an invigorating challenge.

Really smart guys, with various dignified letters after their names, have done all kinds of very intelligent research. These researchers discovered a great truth when they asked people how much they needed to earn to live comfortably. Invariably, respondents listed a desired income roughly 10 percent higher than the income they presently had.

It didn't seem to matter at all how much people made. They all felt they needed 10 percent more to live comfortably. Think about it. If you need 10 percent more than you make each year, you never have enough to live comfortably—even if you make gadzillions.

There is a simple way to get around this universal handicap. Instead of spending 10 percent more than you make, you can save, or pay yourself, 10 percent of everything you make. The only way to do this is to start living on less. It doesn't matter if you make $20 zillion or $20 thousand a year—the principle is the same. Most people in this world live on less than we do. They survive and thrive, and so can we.

We've been brainwashed to believe that spending money to acquire more things will make us happy, when in reality more possessions equal greater worries, higher taxes, increased insurance payments, more responsibilities, unending repair bills, snobby neighbors, and a heck of a lot more surface area that needs dusting, supervising, or getting ulcers over. We become concerned with losing what we have, improving what we have, adding to what we have, or someone stealing what we have. Stuff breaks. Material wealth is heaviness.

Greater freedom to control our time and stress is the ultimate wealth. If we work on changing our desire to get more and more stuff to a increased desire to serve and spend more time with those we love, our ride through life will be a lot more fun. Too often we rationalize our work habits and promise to spend more time with our children, spouses, parents, and friends . . . *tomorrow,* after the orthodontist is paid off, when we buy that new car, after we've moved into our dream home, or when we retire. Doesn't happen. Life, right now, is all we have. Today is as good as it gets.

When we're on our death beds, I don't believe many of us will say, "Gee whiz, I wish I'd spent more time at the office."

2. Don't Lose What You Save

With the possible exception of paying for an education, buying your first home, or making sound business investments, make it a goal to avoid debt. Period. When we discipline ourselves to pay cash instead of making monthly payments, it is amazing how our resourcefulness reawakens and our priorities change.

When we discipline ourselves to save for the entire purchase price of any item, we are much less likely to lose what we save. Saving before we buy gives us firsthand knowledge about the sacrifice in time and effort we exchanged for the item. Those who pay cash for desired possessions are more likely to make wise choices (and understand the difference between wants and needs) than those who borrow the money and pay the price later—plus interest. It is difficult to save fast enough if interest payments on our acquired debt are eating up more of our financial resources than we're able to save.

If we, first, consistently spend less than we earn and, second, don't lose what we save by making wiser choices, we can have the financial freedom to decide how and where to more effectively use our time. My daughter Arianne's desire to own a doll named Samantha illustrates both principles.

Arianne, who is twelve years old, absolutely adores dolls. Someone in marketing found out, because every month or two they send Arianne a full-color catalog filled with pictures of the beautiful "American Girls" doll collection. Problem is, the least expensive doll runs $82, plus $8.95 for shipping and handling. Gift-wrapping is $3 extra, for a grand total of $93.95. That amount is roughly $93 more than Arianne usually has in her possession.

Arianne has dreamed about owning one of those dolls for more than a year. She has pored over the catalog for hours at a time and cut out the pictures to use as homemade paper dolls. Arianne is an intelligent, resourceful child. Her drive to acquire an "American Girls" doll resulted in a series of strategies that are remarkably like the adult money games most of us play. I believe we could learn much from her efforts.

Strategy #1: Creative Noncash Bartering. Arianne wrote to the Pleasant Company and volunteered to help with the fashion show they were sponsoring in our state; she also offered to perform any other work they had so she could earn one of the dolls. No such luck. The company wrote back and told her to come up with the cold, hard cash. Later, Arianne wrote them a letter expressing her concern that this company would produce dolls that were so hard for the average little girl to afford. The Pleasant Company didn't respond pleasantly.

Strategy #2: Saving. Arianne decided if cold, hard cash was the only way she could acquire the doll, she'd better start saving. So she saved and saved and saved. She saved every hint of money that came into her hands. She saved her entire allowance (exactly $2 a week), her babysitting money, and the little extra cash she received when she helped her brother with his newspaper route. By Christmas time, her savings totalled a whopping $27.84. Arianne was getting discouraged. She figured out how long it would take her to save enough money and decided to try a new strategy.

Strategy #3: Outside Income Sources. Since saving was taking too long, Arianne looked at the calendar and decided that December was a good time to try another strategy. She made her Christmas wish list and handed it to her father and me one evening. There was only one thing on the list: her favorite doll from the catalog, "Samantha."

We wanted to buy that doll for Arianne, but she had seven siblings who were trying out the same strategy that month. Arianne did receive a porcelain doll we found on special at Smith's Food and Drug. She seemed pleased, but she kept poring over those catalogs by the hour.

Strategy #4: Loans. Later, I heard Arianne talking to her brother one afternoon. She made him a proposition. She told him if he let her borrow the money to pay for the doll, she would pay him back as soon as possible. Jordan, who is also developing money-making strategies at this point, told Arianne he would be happy to loan her the money if she paid him interest. Arianne didn't understand what interest meant, so Jordan filled her in.

"Interest means you have to pay me back more than you borrowed," Jordan said.

"What? Are you crazy? Do you think I'm dumb or something. That's not a good deal. Thanks, but no thanks," Arianne answered.

Strategy #5: Increase Business. Arianne's babysitting opportunities unexpectedly took a real upswing after Christmas when she took advantage of the babysitting offers her older sisters were too busy for. A homemade flyer, delivered door to door in the neighborhood, also helped build the babysitting business.

By May, Arianne had saved $94. When she told me the news, I was delighted.

"Well, Arianne, good for you! You did it. You finally have enough to buy that doll you've been dreaming about."

"Mom," Arianne answered. "It took me a very *long* time to save this money. I don't want to blow it all on one doll!"

Arianne's money strategies are much like those we adults use when we want something. Interesting things happen when we truly understand wants versus needs and make a commitment to save and pay cash.

The fact is, money represents a means of exchange or a way to get to what you want. (Remember: If the only things we want can be bought with money, our dreams come pretty cheap.) Contrary to popular wisdom, you don't have to earn more each year to increase your net worth or to be happy. In the long run, careful money management is more important than income. If you have problems handling your money when you don't have much, you will have the same problems when you have much more.

By our thirties, most of us have faced the reality of full-time employment, home mortgages, car payments, children, and braces. Our dreams have changed from solving the world's hunger problems to figuring out a way to solve *our* hunger problem and lose weight. Our mountain of debt has reached such a height we can't see any possible way to dig out. We've all been told many times over that money won't buy us happiness—but we're usually more than willing to hang in there and give it a second chance.

Herein lies the answer: **If you're in a hole, you need to quit digging it deeper.** You don't give up your dreams or plans—you just have to give up your debt.

"I know where every penny goes," a middle-level business manager told me the other day. "I have our entire budget on a fancy computer program. So why are we having such a hard time making ends meet? I make a good salary, but my wife had to take a temporary part-time job at minimum wage just to get the kids in school. We're behind on our house and car payments. We need more money."

Most of us sincerely believe the answer to our financial dissatisfaction is a larger income. Making more money is seldom the answer. The answer lies in learning to be more satisfied with what we already have and developing new ways to make the best use of what we have.

DON'T BE FOOLED BY THE MYTHS

A lot of false myths about money have been circulating for centuries. One is that a little more money will solve our problems. In truth, in most cases a little more money actually increases problems. For instance, when I finally earned enough to buy some new carpet for our home, I suddenly developed "new carpet paranoia." I insisted the children take off their shoes when they came inside, kept a constant vigil at the dinner table for spilled fruit punch, and straddled the carpeted stairs so I wouldn't create a trail by walking up the center. Life with my old carpet was much less of a problem.

Another popular myth is that spending money on our appetites and passions will satisfy them. Well, I can't remember the last time I was able to eat *one* potato chip. Many of us believe times are different now—only fools pay taxes and the road to financial freedom is paved with debt. Not so. Hard work, living providently, and avoiding debt still constitute the most sure road to financial freedom.

Part of the good news about our money is that, compared to almost everybody else in the world—and many of them are very happy—we already have more than most. The trick is in learning to savor it. Money simply does not come with instructions. More money just makes things more complicated, particularly if you don't manage it wisely. The principles of money management don't change, whether you have a little or a lot to work with. The trick to successfully managing your money is in successfully managing yourself.

BUDGETING: SEPARATING WANTS FROM NEEDS

Budgeting is the door to freedom for people with the vision to separate their wants from their needs. We *need* nourishing food, adequate shelter, and durable clothing. We *want* Hostess Cupcakes, lavish homes in the best neighborhoods, and twenty-seven pairs of designer-name athletic shoes with inflatable soles and blinking shoelaces. The problem with most wants is, once we get them, we usually want more.

Budgeting, simply put, is figuring out what your income is and then deciding how to spend it *before* you acquire a bill or run to the store. Developing and using a family budget means taking charge of your resources and becoming the owners of an official family spending plan. Most of us will manage over a million dollars during the forty or so years we're in the work force. It makes sense to plan our spending before our spending makes plans for us.

Families, like businesses, need some form of spending control and long-range planning or they go broke. Families, unlike businesses, ought to operate on more than just the bottom line. Families can become so budget conscious that they never spend their money joyously or spontaneously. Balanced budgeting is spending with our heads and our hearts.

When Ross and I were first married, we lived near a widow who had a very comfortable retirement. This widow could sense that Ross and I would not have trouble budgeting and saving, but she worried we might make the same mistake she and her husband had years ago.

"My husband and I were so busy planning for the future that we forgot to enjoy our lives together," the widow told me. "Six weeks before he was to retire, my husband died. I can count on one hand the vacations he had taken in his life. We seldom spent money on gifts for each other. We stretched every dollar for the basic necessities and saved every penny we could for retirement. Now I have all the money I could ever want and no husband to enjoy it with. Don't spend so much time saving for the future that you forget to live and love today."

This widow taught me that wise family budgets should include planning for the future without neglecting the family's need to enjoy part of the resources today. Financial freedom has as much to do with traveling in a balanced way as it does with aiming for the right destination. The key is *balance*. Choose the direction in which you want to travel, but make sure you're able to enjoy the ride along the way.

The best way to begin a workable family budget, then, is not to start with your wants or even with the money you have available. Instead, you ought to start by forcing yourself to write down what you desire. It's downright essential that you understand your own heartfelt desires first—then you can make effective plans and begin to enjoy the journey. No amount of money will ever satisfy you if you don't know what you most desire.

The next step in budgeting is to monitor your money. You need to know what your income is, and you need to track your spending over a specified period. The easiest way to do this is to record all expenditures in a small notebook, or put them on a computer program. Any method will work. The idea is to know how much money you have to work with and where your money is going, right now.

Another important step in making a successful budget is to involve all family members in the planning stages. Family members who feel they have some control over the family financial pie are more likely to develop some self-control over pie snarfing. For example, if the children are aware that money is being saved for a family vacation in the summer, they are more willing to go without a few treats and movies today.

At our family budget meetings we list or estimate income for the budgeting period, which includes monthly and yearly expenses. Then we total our income and outgo with a eagle eye for cutting or adjusting discretionary expenditures. We explore new ways to make do with less. The simplest budgeting method we've used includes the following elements:

1. Having the bank automatically withdraw a set amount from the checking account to deposit in the savings account (savings are divided into short term, long term, and retirement);

2. Paying for set bills with checks;

3. Withdrawing a predetermined amount of cash for everything else we will need that week. When the cash runs out, we stop spending.

My husband, Ross, was totally unimpressed when I enthusiastically showed him all the money I saved by buying several pieces of clothing on sale at a local department store one day after our cash was gone.

"Look at these prices," I said excitedly. "I really saved us a lot of money today."

"Janene," Ross said matter-of-factly, "you never save money by spending it."

In truth, *everyone* has to control their spending. Even rich guys choose between a villa by the sea or a chalet in the mountains. There will never be enough money for everything. We all make spending choices that will eventually limit other choices.

All you really need to set up a workable family budget is a piece of paper, a pencil, and a desire to try. The rewards that come from following a budget or spending plan include a sense of control, self-reliance during emergencies, and having the means to pay for education, health care, and insurance, as well as financial independence and the ability to stay out of bankruptcy court or prison.

When developing a balanced family budget, it helps me to remember that all my family members have their own "money personality." Some members are risk takers, while others are conservative. Some people like to feel in control of their money, while others like to wing it. Some people like to buy *things* like homes, furniture, and cars, while others like to buy *experiences* like vacations, classes, or hobbies. Once you understand the money personality of each family member (including yourself), you can better communicate your financial goals and plans, without a hidden agenda.

Most of us also have a wish list of things we would like to own, or experiences we would like to have. Family budgets run a little smoother when those wish lists are put on paper and prioritized. For example, if the wife would like a new refrigerator before anything else, but the husband would like a new lawn mower, and the children would like a summer vacation, it's time for a family fight or the fine art of compromise.

"Let's see," the husband says, "I'll agree to put the new refrigerator first on our list if you agree to purchase a model under a certain amount." Or, "Let's see," the wife says, "I'll agree to put the lawn mower first on the wish list if you agree to set aside $50 a month toward the refrigerator." Or, "Let's see," the children say, "we'll agree to a camping trip instead of Disneyland, if Dad will promise not to make us go on long, predawn hikes devoid of restrooms."

Many couples have one spouse, better known as Master-of-de-Money, who takes over all financial affairs. Family life works much better if *both* spouses are fully aware of income and investments, taxes, and expenses and have equal voice in all financial decisions. We don't do anyone any favors when we assume full responsibility for something that should be jointly shared by both husband and wife, whether it is child care, household chores, or family finances. Everybody has to grow up and smell the roses eventually.

You may never get the bathroom painted, but you'll work more as a team and view money more as a means to an end if you budget your money. It doesn't matter what shape or form the family budget takes, as long as the entire family is part of the agreement and makes a true effort to stick to the plan.

USING CREDIT WISELY

People spend borrowed money less carefully than earned money. It wasn't too long ago that families would not even consider buying something unless they had the money to pay for it. Today, many couples use credit like a child in a candy store. Total price for any item is seldom understood, and monthly payments are considered a necessary evil.

Monthly payments are advertised as a way for you to afford to pay for things you can't afford. In truth, monthly payments mean you paid extra for something you couldn't afford in the first place, because you pay for the item plus interest. The smartest move is to avoid using credit entirely.

If we are going to use credit, we should do so wisely, which means we have to understand it. Before I married a banker, I believed money lenders, such as banks, had lots of cash in a vault on site and that money borrowers, like me, just dropped by and picked up some money with a smile and a promise to be good and pay it back according to schedule. I know a little more about credit now, but the basics stay the same.

Using credit means borrowing money, getting a loan, or using a credit card. Every time you use credit, you develop or add to your financial reputation. You build good credit by paying your bills on time. When you have good credit, you can borrow and charge as you need to.

The credit bureau collects incriminating information on consumers. Any time you apply for credit, the bank or store will check with the credit bureau. If you didn't pay back a loan or you typically pay late, you have poor credit and won't get your loan or charge account. If you want to maintain a good credit rating, you have to pay your bills, and you have to do so on time. When you don't pay your bills, terrible, horrible, no good, very bad, awful things happen.

So, it pays *not* to:

• write checks for more money than you have in your checking account,

• use charge cards when you don't have enough money to cover the purchase,

• use your savings for day-to-day living expenses, and

• have your monthly budget so tight that you don't leave room for the unexpected, like the water heater blowing up in the middle of the night.

Most of us know these don'ts, but we're not able to look far enough ahead to see the results of our failure to follow them. For instance, breaking a lease can land you in court, cost you thousands of dollars, and give you a major headache. When you sign a lease, you are obligated to pay rent until a certain date. Even if you move out early, you are still obligated to pay that rent. If your landlord sues, you will lose your sleep as well as your shirt. If you stay in the building but don't pay the landlord, he or she can start legal action to throw you out.

If you don't pay for electricity, water, or telephone, your service will be disconnected. If you don't repay your car loan, the bank can repossess the car in the dark of night and sell it. You lose the car, plus all the money you paid on it, plus your good credit. If you owe money and a creditor takes you to court, you will lose. You will have to pay what you owe, as well as court costs, legal fees, and expenses.

If the bank repossesses the assets used for collateral on the loan and that collateral is not sufficient to pay back the loan, the bank can get a judgment against your other assets for the difference. Contrary to popular opinion, bankers do not like to foreclose on loans because foreclosures cost them money. When you don't pay your loan back in full, you rob other borrowers, who must pay higher interest rates to make up the losses for those who don't pay back their loans. Everybody loses. If you can't pay in any other way, the court can order garnishment of your wages. This means your employer must send part of your paycheck to your creditor until the debt is paid off. Employers don't like this because it costs them time and money. Besides, it makes you look bad.

When money is tight and you have more bills than money, it helps to pay in this order: rent, insurance, utilities, car, and other secured loans. Then move on to doctors, dentists, lenders of unsecured loans, department stores, and mail-order accounts (all these will often take smaller payments for a month or two). Unfortunately, despite your best efforts, the tooth fairy will not wave a magic wand; you will still have to pay all your bills in full, plus all accumulated interest.

When you can't pay, you can contact your creditors to tell them you're aware of the bill, explain how you hope to solve the problem, and send a small payment to show good faith. It helps to tell them when to expect full payment and ask them to work out a repayment plan with you. All of your bills have to be paid. If you don't take action, in a short time these creditors will take action against you.

No matter how tough things get, bankruptcy should always be the last resort. In the end, bankruptcy will usually hurt you more than your creditors will. When you file for bankruptcy, you ask the court to say you can't pay your bills. If the court declares you bankrupt, you do not have to pay your debts. But you lose most of what you own. The court takes it to pay your creditors. It becomes public knowledge that you can't repay what you owe. It will be much more difficult to get loans or any credit in the future because the bankruptcy will stay on your credit record for ten years.

Your job is to figure out what your family truly needs, then find creative ways to eliminate or reduce spending on everything else. For instance, if your house payment is killing you, you can sell the monster and get a smaller place to live—and have less gray hair. You might want a big fancy house, but you don't need it. If you bought the house to impress your family or friends, you need not bother. People love you for the way they feel about themselves when they are in your company. Your ability to love them is what people love about you. If you have a car payment that is strapping you, you can trade the car in, sell it, take the bus, walk, or ride with someone. We all need to be open to alternative ways of providing for our needs before we get in so far over our heads that there is no way out but bankruptcy.

Generally, when we are out of control of our spending, we have a much deeper-seated problem and are using spending to replace something that is missing in our lives. Surveys have shown that married people fight about money more than anything else. Spenders often marry savers, or spouses take on the role of the spender or saver in self-defense. It takes a lot of give and take for couples and families to work out a plan that everyone feels good about. But it's worth it. You exchange some ongoing work and effort—and in return you find *unity* and *freedom*.

CHAPTER 3

Making Our Income a Little Less Gross

Think of your brethren like unto yourselves, and be familiar with all and free with your substance, that they may be rich like unto you.

—Jacob 2:17

GIFTS

Once there was a boy who went to his father and asked for a candy bar.

"Then you must earn a dollar," the father answered.

The boy was confused.

"Just give me a dollar," the boy said.

"You can have a candy bar after you earn a dollar," the boy's father answered.

The boy was angry, but later he went to the grocery store and asked the owner if he could work for a dollar.

The boy went home to his father and said, "I earned a dollar and I bought my own candy bar."

"When you earn more dollars," the father said, "buy three. Eat one, save one, and give one away."

The boy frowned. He believed his father was a foolish old man. The boy went back to the grocery store owner and asked if he could earn more dollars.

Soon the boy had another paycheck. He took it to the grocery store and bought thirty-seven candy bars. That night, alone in his bedroom, the boy ate all the candy bars. The boy felt sick, but it was a sickness in his heart, and not just his stomach.

"Maybe I need new clothes or a new car to make myself feel better," the boy thought to himself. "Maybe I need more than candy bars."

So the boy worked hard, and when he was paid he bought

51

himself many new clothes with labels on the outside and a snazzy new red sports car so all his friends could see.

When none of his friends seemed to notice or care, the boy still felt sick inside.

"Maybe if I become someone important, I will not feel sick inside," the boy thought.

So the boy went to the university and on to medical school. After years and years of school and a lengthy residency, the boy began performing surgery at a hospital in his old hometown.

Some people treated the boy differently now, and the boy liked it. The nurses followed his orders, and (for the most part) his patients were grateful. But sometimes his patients didn't pay their bills, and sometimes his patients sued him for malpractice. The boy felt sick inside.

One day, the boy became very ill. He had to stay in the hospital for many months, and he almost died when his doctor gave him the wrong medicine by mistake. The boy wanted to sue the doctor and the hospital. The boy couldn't pay his bills. He had to sell everything he owned, and he was still sick.

One day when his father came to visit the boy in the hospital, he said, "You have done all you can do. I will make up the difference."

So the father sold his farm and tractor and paid the boy's bills. The father talked to the boy's doctor about the medication mistake and told the doctor that the boy had forgiven him.

Then the boy's father went back to the boy's hospital room and stroked his son's forehead and placed warm blankets around his shoulders. The boy's father read to the boy and slept in a cot next to the boy every night.

The boy wept.

"I cannot accept your gift," the boy said to his father. "I am not worthy. I did not listen to you and follow your instructions. I kept all the candy bars for myself, and I feel sick inside."

"You are my son," the father answered. "I will make up the difference."

Soon the boy became well, but his father was too old and too tired and soon he died.

"I cannot pay my father back," the boy said. "I will have to find someone and do for them what my father did for me."

The boy started a free clinic. He donated money to medical research. He started a candy bar factory.

Each day when the boy woke, he remembered his father and he thought of one more thing he could do. Every day the boy felt good inside. 🙐

NET VERSUS GROSS

I always get confused when people talk to me about net or gross income. Experts tell me that my net income is what is left over after taxes and my gross income is what I start out with. I, on the other hand, say the income I have left over after taxes looks pretty gross.

One technique I've developed to help myself feel better about my income is to remember that part of all I earn is mine to keep. I do this by paying myself at least 10 percent of my income, which helps it seem less gross. Then I also remember that part of all I earn is mine to give away. I do this by giving away at least 10 percent. In my view, a master plan for grossless income includes owning a saving and giving plan.

PART OF ALL I EARN IS MINE TO GIVE AWAY

We make a living with what we get. We make a life with what we give away. One of the most neglected purposes of money is to increase our ability to serve other people. When we decide to give of ourselves, along with our possessions, we reap the benefits of increased physical well-being, emotional happiness, and spiritual harmony. If you ask me, that's a pretty good bargain. We can heal ourselves when we reach out to others.

Most of us choose to focus on what we don't have. We work a lifetime for bigger houses, newer cars, nicer clothes, and foreign travel—then wonder why we still feel empty and dissatisfied. We forget that a truly successful life requires the giving and receiving of unconditional love. While materialism seems attractive, a truly meaningful life always nurtures spirituality. Spirituality involves living an other-centered life and requires us to treat other human beings the same way we want them to treat us. The secret of life is discovering that the three things most of us desire—happiness, freedom, and peace of mind—can be ours only if we give them to someone else.

We are never truly prosperous until we are able to give away our money and our time. Our minds and hearts make us rich. If we consistently give away at least 10 percent of our total income as a tithe, we are transforming our character. (And if we consistently give ourselves at least 10 percent by saving, we are transforming our possibilities.)

Americans enjoy one of the highest standards of living in the world. Yet most of us are also in debt up to our eyeballs and seldom have a spare dollar to spend or give away. We rarely think of our income as a means to help anyone besides ourselves. When we do give, if we're honest with ourselves, most of us have expectation of reward. Real giving doesn't expect or even hope for a return. The best givers have short memories. They give with joy, and that very joy is their reward. Some recognize gifts everywhere; their gratitude is their reward. Only what we give away is truly ours to keep.

The guy with the most stuff still dies. What we can't give away owns us, because we have to tend and take care of it.

Then again, the best gifts we give have nothing to do with possessions. The greatest gifts I have received are forgiveness, tolerance, charity, and respect. There is no greater joy in life than that which comes from freely giving and receiving love.

PART OF ALL I EARN IS MINE TO KEEP

On the other side of the equation, we can all give ourselves peace of mind simply by saving. Our supply of money is finite and limited; there is not enough for everything. When we use our money for one thing, we eliminate the possibility of using it for another thing. The need for making choices is not eliminated by increased income. No matter how much we make, there will never be enough for everything.

If we are wise, our family financial goals and priorities will include those things that are most important to us. That's why it is so important to decide, early in life, what is truly important. This involves learning to see life as it really is. When we decide not to spend money on things that don't matter, we can save for things that do. When we give our money to ourselves by saving, we've allowed the miracle of the loaves and the fishes to enter our lives. The more we save, the more we have to give ourselves and others.

Our income is basically allocated to fixed bills, savings for short-term stuff, and savings for stuff way out there in the future. One of the best reasons to save is to provide ourselves with an emergency fund so that we don't have a coronary when we're hit over the head with the unexpected events like unemployment or medical emergencies. Bad things do happen to good people. We can't stop bad things from happening, but we can prepare for them. For example, it is prudent planning to set aside three to six months' salary in a liquid savings account for unexpected emergencies.

Another reason to save is to provide us with the money to pay cash for the expensive things we want. If we discipline ourselves to put away regular amounts for a car or other large purchase, we'll be able to buy with cash and save ourselves the hefty finance changes. When we want to buy new stuff like couches or refrigerators, it's always best to pay for them with cash. I've noticed when I force myself to save the entire amount before I make a purchase, something weird happens. Sometimes I decide I don't really want the stuff after all.

In addition to saving for the things we want today or next year, it makes sense to save for the things we want twenty years from now. Long-term saving plans are required for homes, missions, weddings, college education, and retirement. For long-term saving, we need to take into account what inflation will do with our savings. There are better forms of saving for retirement than simple saving accounts—consider IRAs and employer-assisted retirement plans. These types of retirement plans are tax deferred and are probably the most painless way to save over the long haul. Some individuals prefer to buy income property as a hedge against inflation.

It's not how much you have to save that matters. What matters is that you do save, at least a little, from all your income. When you put savings in a savings account, the money begins drawing interest. That small amount of interest begins to draw its own interest. This accumulation of interest paid on interest, compound interest, means the entire account grows faster and faster. The sooner you start saving, the more time compound interest has to weave its magic.

There's only one major problem with savings plans. You have to have money to save. Ah, there's the rub. Some people find an automatic payroll deduction the easiest way to force themselves to save. We have our payroll department deposit our paycheck directly to our checking account, then have the bank transfer a specific amount to our savings account before we ever get our hands on it. Some people find it helpful to reduce the number of dependents they claim as tax exemptions so that more money is withheld from their salary for taxes. When they get their tax refund, the money goes straight into savings. It doesn't matter how you find the money to save, as long as you do it consistently.

Insurance payments can also be considered a form of saving for the unexpected. Families face thousands of dollars of potential debt when they have no health, car, personal property, and life insurance. I view insurance as a way for me to pay for all the really awful stuff that could happen that I wouldn't be able to pay for out-of-pocket.

If you're a parent with dependent children, you need life insurance. All wage earners with dependents need adequate life and disability insurance to cover the needs of their family in the event of their disability or death. Insurance is especially important for single parents or those who are the primary wage earner. Parents who do not work outside the home also need insurance to pay for funeral expenses, child care, and housekeeping expenses that would need to be purchased in the event of their death.

When you're unmarried and without children, you need little if any life insurance. If you're retired with grown children, you can probably do without much life insurance, unless you're going to pass on a large estate to your heirs and want insurance to pay the estate taxes.

Statistics tell us that many of us will have to handle all our financial affairs alone someday. We can't blindly hope our spouses will outlive us and take care of us. We have to take the responsibility to study up on Social Security benefits, retirement and pension plans, savings accounts, home mortgages, stocks, bonds, different types of life insurance, wills, and burial arrangements. Part of being an adult is assuming the financial responsibility for ourselves. (Appendix A consists of a few financial definitions to get you started.)

It's also a good idea for both spouses to have their own personal checking and/or savings accounts and to secure one or more credit cards in his or her name alone. We need to be aware of all our family financial records, including such things as checking account numbers, credit card numbers, insurance policies, safe-deposit box keys, business and brokerage records, tax returns, and company books. Financial knowledge and independence for both spouses is especially important if one of them usually makes the majority of the family income and financial decisions.

Whether we work inside or outside the home right now, we need the skills or education to financially provide for our families, if the need arises. Divorce, disability, separation, death, bankruptcy, or any of a number of life events may require the need for employment at the most unexpected times. A good education and up-to-date career training can be considered another form of insurance.

I vividly remember glancing around the table at my six young children (eight years of age and under) one morning during breakfast and realizing I was not adequately prepared to provide for them if I had to become the sole breadwinner. That's when I decided to go back to school, finish my degree, and begin my own home-based business. I've never regretted that decision.

Another great way to save is to reduce what we need to spend. Saving on the necessities of life by reducing our expenses will not only build our savings account but will build our creativity and resourcefulness as well.

"Use it up, wear it out, make it do, or do without" is a favorite saying from my parents' generation, and it still holds true today. All of us need housing, food, and clothing. Most of us, at some time, need health care and a form of transportation. Saving money on these necessities is not only possible but essential if we ever want to get out and stay out of debt. I know it sounds boring and self-sacrificing, but actually saving money on the necessities of life can be a great and enjoyable challenge.

SAVING MONEY ON FOOD

I know a man who found a terrific way to save money on the family grocery bill. Every night he'd pay his kids $1 each if they'd go to bed without supper. Then, in the morning, he'd charge them $1 apiece for breakfast.

I know how the guy feels.

Another fellow I know said he just about had his children trained not to eat, but they up and died on him.

"If you kids would quit eating, we'd have a lot more food around here," I spouted the other day.

My husband and I often have total strangers walk up to us in the supermarket, peer into our grocery cart, count our thirteen gallons of milk, and say things like, "Boy, you folks ought to get a cow!"

When I go to the refrigerator searching for a little supper menu inspiration, what I usually find is wilted lettuce leaves, empty milk containers, iceless cube trays, and somebody's science fair project stinking up the whole joint. The other night, when I opened the refrigerator to locate supper, it wasn't there. After intense interrogation, I located the carrots in April, the milk in Ashley, the pudding in Arianne, the casserole in Aubrey, the pickles in Jacob, the bread in Joseph, the cheese in Amy, and the celery in Jordan.

Feeding a family is a thankless task because, let's face it, every time you cook something somebody eats it and you have to start all over. Even with all the bother of working for money to buy food, shopping for food, cooking food, and cleaning up after food, eating is an important part of the family budget and a great way to make pleasant memories.

Most of the people on this planet work hard every day just to get something to eat. Americans are blessed with an abundant, inexpensive food supply. Americans spend a smaller percentage of the family income on food than any other country. The nice thing is, you don't have to be rich to enjoy good food. We can enjoy the same potato rich people do, less one fancy tuxedoed waiter. I don't believe rich people eat better food than us regular folks. I tried those snails once and we're not missing anything.

Even though food is relatively inexpensive, there are still many ways to cut your food bill without cutting back on nutrition. For instance, one of the best and least known ways to cut back on grocery bills (and weight gain) is to cut back on sweets and prepared snack foods. On the other hand, many convenience foods, considered a luxury by some, cost less than home-prepared items and save time. For example, day-old bread at the bakery thrift store is cheaper to buy than bread made at home.

Food manufacturers and retailers spend millions of dollars

figuring out how to entice us to spend more money at the grocery store. Marketing studies have been done to see what overhead music keeps people in the store the longest, what colors are best for the food item's package, and where to place high-profit products to increase sales. Children also spend millions of hours figuring out how to entice parents to spend more money at the grocery store. While we are asleep at night, our kids complete marketing studies about what screaming pitch in the store will most embarrass us into buying more candy and how to quickly rip open packages so that we feel obligated to buy them. Feeding a family takes real bravery, cunning, and skill.

Entering a grocery store is much like going on a jungle safari. It's a wild adventure, and only the best prepared come out alive. The best hunters know their way around the jungle, and the best food shoppers know their way around the grocery store. Ever wondered why you have to use a machete to cut through thousands of products before you can get a gallon of milk? Grocery stores are arranged in such a way as to force shoppers to hike through willpower busters like candy and cookies in order to get to the good stuff at the end of the trail, like milk or fresh produce.

Willpower busters have less power over us when we make a list of what we need before we get to the store. On the other hand, if we're too tied to a list, we might neglect to take advantage of in-store specials on items we regularly buy. Some people like to prepare their shopping list from a week's or month's worth of menus. I prefer to make a shopping list from the week's grocery ads and figure out my menus from the best buys.

Good food hunters are also aware of seasonal deals. When food is in season and the supply is abundant, cost goes down. The fine art of food hunting can be even more enjoyable when we use our backyards to raise our own animals or to cultivate a vegetable and fruit garden. My husband and I have grown a garden for the past twenty years. Half the fun of our summer has come in snitching green peas, gathering eggs, slicing a plateful of juicy, home-grown tomatoes, and munching away on hot, butter-dripping corn, fresh on the cob.

If a hunter wants his game processed or stuffed to hang on the wall, it costs money. It works the same way with food shopping. Packaging and processing add to the cost. For example, rolled oats cost a fraction of the price of processed oat breakfast cereal. Fresh produce costs a fraction of the price of canned or frozen. Each time someone handles the food item, a profit must be made, so it helps to buy the food directly from the producer. For example, if we buy our meat from the guy who raises the animal, and then have it cut and wrapped, we'll save. Once we get to the grocery store, the same principle applies. Every time an item of food goes through one more processing step, it adds to the final cost. For example, a whole turkey costs much less per pound than turkey steaks (though with the steaks there is much less wastage). We have to decide if the convenience of pre-prepared foods is worth the cost.

Successful food hunting trips take planning. Each time we run to the store for a gallon of milk, we may forget the milk and end up spending money on Ding-Dongs. The fewer trips we make to the grocery store, the less we'll spend. If our local grocery stores are located near each other, it may be worth our time to shop the specials at each store. Yet if we pay more than we save for the gas to chase around, then it doesn't make sense. It really helps the family food budget to limit major grocery shopping trips to once or twice a month, with small in-between trips to buy milk and fresh produce.

Experienced hunters rarely take novices along to step on twigs and scare the game in the area. Experienced shoppers rarely take along children or spouses when hunting groceries. Food hunting professionals also remember to eat before they shop, buy items in bulk when they find them on sale, and stay on the lookout for unusual or discount food stores. Day-old bread and pastry stores, along with warehouse stores that sell perishable foods that are past code or near code (meaning, they are threatening to become stale or overripe), can also help.

Food hunters on a budget also understand the real cost of any meal eaten away from home—including tip, gas to get there and back, and the babysitter. Most meals out will typically cost four times the amount the same meal would cost if prepared at home. Unlike game hunters, who are forced to eat out on the trail, families are better off limiting restaurant meals to special events like birthdays. Eating good food in a nice atmosphere with someone else doing the work is one of life's pleasures, but doing so on a regular basis represents a choice between this pleasure and using that money for something else we might also enjoy. Picnic basket candlelight dinners at the park or in the mountains, barbecues in the backyard, and bike-ride sack lunches are creative, inexpensive alternatives to more expensive restaurant meals.

If a hunter doesn't take the time to carefully look through his sight on the rifle, he loses an accurate aim on his target. Many families lose sight of the dollars spent on fast food, such as hamburgers, malts, pizza, soft drinks, hot dogs, tacos, and other food eaten away from home.

Experienced shoppers know their generic brands and understand that coupons are a good deal only when they are for items they normally buy. Good shoppers often join a food co-op, where they can get food for reduced prices.

Hunting parties keep their base camp well stocked with the necessities, and good food shoppers keep their pantries well stocked with the basics. A year's supply of food is great security in times of need or disaster, but it is also a great hedge against inflation. Most families can't afford to buy, or find the place to store, all the food their family would normally consume in one year. But most families, if motivated, can buy a year's supply of basic, life-sustaining food for one year.

Once we've tamed the adventures of the jungle called grocery shopping, it helps to understand the people we're shopping for. I offer the following condensed version of expert versus realistic advice for parents abandoned in the rough and dirty trenches sometimes referred to as the family feeding hour:

Expert advice: "Parents should feed their newborns on demand. Rigid schedules are frustrating to both the child and parent."

Realistic advice: "Newborns expect to eat approximately 23.99 hours per day. The rest of your time will be spent diapering and burping. New parents generally secure about .000001 hours of sleep per night if baby isn't fussy."

Expert advice: "Parents should allow their children to experiment with their food and explore the wonder of color, texture, and flavor."

Realistic advice: "Color coordinate your dinner menu with the color of your toddler's clothing. This means if your little tyke is wearing red, spaghetti is a possibility, but only if you're suffering from acute memory loss. If your child is wearing light-colored clothing, serve water, celery, and white bread. When serving purple pudding or sauce, strip child, then secure garden hose and steel wool pad."

Expert advice: "Don't allow mealtimes to become a war zone. Children will eventually consume a balanced diet if left alone without adult supervision and given the freedom to choose for themselves."

Realistic advice: "School-age children and cows have a lot in common—they both graze all day, burp without saying, 'excuse me,' and come complete with about sixteen stomachs."

Expert advice: "It is vital that adolescents follow healthy eating habits during this important growth period of their lives. The entire physical health of the future generation depends on what your teens eat today."

Realistic advice: "Teens are black holes. They either live on air or they eat it, along with everything else in sight. But don't surrender yet. There are better days ahead. Before you know it, your children will grow up and bring home grandchildren to furnish you with a refresher boot camp on the heroic art of feeding the troops."

Sometimes food and families seem to make a difficult mix. But there are times when it all seems worth it. There's something about looking around the table at your wild and wonderful family—throwing food, elbowing each other, and spilling their milk—that gets to you somewhere inside and tells you that you are going to go crazy . . . but someday, too soon, your family mealtimes will be peaceful and boring once again.

SAVING MONEY ON HEALTH CARE

"Mom, you really need to get in shape," my health-conscious daughter, Aubrey, said.

"Aubrey," I answered, "round is a shape."

The bottom line in health care is that we need to do everything we can to keep ourselves healthy in the first place. When we do get sick, we need to do what we can to help ourselves get better. If we need help, it pays to find the best deal on health care. If we're troubled by chronic conditions, we need to learn to stay happy so we can cope with our health problems.

Whether the government has a large or small stake in our health care, we all benefit when costs are controlled. That means, in large part, that we must prevent problems in the first place. Studies report that medical care affects less than 10 percent of our health. The other 90 percent is affected by our knowledge and accident awareness, our environment (pollution and water), and our choices in nutrition, smoking, alcohol, drugs, and sanitation. There are real economic (as well as physical and spiritual) benefits that come from healthy living habits.

Staying Healthy

One of the most important but least understood parts of a family wellness plan is to develop our sixth sense, which is our sense of humor. Careful research shows that if we suppress laughter, it sucks back down into our body and spreads out at our hips. If we can find humor in a problem, we can survive it.

Stress levels can also be managed with humor. When we laugh, blood pressure drops, breathing slows, muscular tension subsides, and we generally feel better. Laughing many times a day is like a good cardiovascular workout. A growing body of evidence supports the idea that humor is good for your health. Biochemically, laughter seems to cause the release of natural painkillers that combat arthritis and other inflammatory conditions and slow the release of some stress hormones. Humor is really the communication of insight. So if we don't have a sense of humor, we may not have much sense at all.

Another way to stay healthy is by keeping a journal. Journal writing is like soul jogging. A journal is a way to create meaning in our lives through self-discovery. Journals provide us with a solitary journey to find out what we, as individuals, feel and think. Through the process of writing in our journals regularly, we can change the way we view our lives. From the writing of familiar, ordinary events, we come to know ourselves. When we record our frustrations it becomes more difficult to live in anger or denial, because we develop an increased clarity about our own needs and motives. Writing in a journal is extremely important to our emotional and spiritual health.

Exercising to stay well may seem like a pain, but it's a life saver. Exercise affects our self-esteem, helps us unclutter our minds, and releases our creativity. Exercise has a positive effect on mild depression, and decreases anger, fatigue, and confusion. Exercise increases our sense of well-being and decreases PMS symptoms, muscle tension, blood pressure, and anxiety.

Eating a well-balanced diet and getting adequate rest are important, but it's not necessary to look like a magazine cover model to look and feel good at a healthy weight. Everyone has his or her own genetic coding, and it's important to love the body you have. When you can tell your weight is stopping you from doing things that bring you joy, it's probably time to do something about it.

Many of us rush to the doctor when we could successfully treat the health problem at home. A good medical reference book is one of the best health-care investments we can make. These books don't replace our doctors, but they help us decide whether or not we need one by pointing out the differences between what is serious and what is not.

Some adult screening tests have proven helpful in detecting life-threatening problems, but running to the doctor every other day isn't necessary. Doctors and clinics are happy to supply us with screening guidelines on such things as Pap smears and blood tests, and tests for colon cancer, breast cancer, high cholesterol, high blood pressure, and diabetes.

As a rule, we don't need frequent checkups if we feel well, except for a few specific tests. Blood pressure tests, Pap smears, breast examinations, glaucoma testing, and dental checks are the most important. Everyone needs a plan for obtaining medical care before the need arises, but elaborate physical examinations can uncover abnormalities that worry us without cause, especially if we're a little paranoid to start with.

When We Get Sick

Even after all we can do to keep ourselves well, most of us get sick and need help getting better. The medical guys don't have all the answers, but they have some of them and can be a great help. Doctors are human beings. Some are better at what they do than others. We need to make wise choices when we use the medical establishment and remember that when we go to a doctor's office or a medical facility, *we* are in charge.

In the ideal situation, doctors and patients are partners. But in the real world, many patients are afraid to challenge medical authority. Many patients won't speak up because they don't understand the medical lingo and are too embarrassed to say so. In reality, patients who ask questions are generally perceived as intelligent people who are involved in their own care. Health-care professionals take us more seriously when we are involved.

If we want a good deal in health care, we need to think of our doctor visit much as we would an interview session with a reporter at our local newspaper. The doctor wants to know the *story* of our problem. He or she will want to know (1) *what* the problem is, (2) *when* the problem began, and (3) a little more background information about our health in general, such as family history, hospitalizations, operations, allergies, and medications. Next, doctors usually review symptoms related to other body systems, though seemingly unrelated to our complaint. Finally, doctors want some information on our lifestyle.

It always helps to start with the symptom that bothers us the most. Many patients go to a doctor with several problems and leave until last the symptom that concerns them the most—when the doctor is hanging on the doorknob. If we mention the most troubling problem first, the doctor is better able to focus on our real needs.

To get a good deal from a routine doctor visit, we have to write down questions before we go. Here are some you may want to ask:

"How much will this office visit and prescription cost me?"

(Yes, we may actually discuss fees with our doctors. Many doctors insulate themselves from the business end of their work and need frequent reminders.)

"Is this a common problem?"

(It might help us to know that there are thousands of other people with the same problem.)

"What does the diagnosis mean?"

(Doctors speak English, if we make them. We might have to tack their thumbs to the wall, but we don't have to let them leave until we understand what they said to us.)

"Could the problem be anything else?"

(A doctor's first opinion on a problem is just that, his first opinion. Make him think a little deeper. We're paying for this, remember.)

"What do I need to do now?"

(It's amazing how many patients walk away from a visit to the doctor with their mouths open and their brains on fuzz-out. We need to get the doctor to tell us clearly what we need to do after the visit, then do it.)

"Is there anything I should not do?"

(No, the doctor didn't tell me not to jump on a trampoline after giving birth, but I should have asked.)

"When should I check back with you?"

(Many problems don't go away after the first treatment, and we need to know when and if the doctor will need to see us again.)

"What can I do to keep this problem from recurring?"

(Many problems are caused by things we are doing or not doing. We need to find out how to help ourselves from becoming repeat offenders.)

"Where can I go for a second opinion?"

(No, the doctor is not all knowing and powerful. Yes, we may need to seek another qualified doctor to give us a second opinion.)

"Did you wash your hands?"

(Health-care providers should wash and put gloves on in our presence.)

Whenever a doctor prescribes a medication, you should ask him or her if there is any alternate or generic drug that costs less. U. S. Food and Drug Administration approval guarantees the same standards of purity, quality, and strength for generic brands as brand names. You can do your part in keeping costs down when you choose the least expensive and most convenient pharmacy, then remember to comparison shop.

The most frequently prescribed medications in the United States are tranquilizers, minor pain relievers, and sedatives. These drugs seldom, if ever, solve any medical condition, often put a mask over the true problem, and cause the greatest number of side effects. This prescription pattern arose because consumers demanded it. You can decrease the cost of medications by eliminating or decreasing your demands for medications you don't really need. (Of course, there are legitimate uses for these medications, especially in the short term. But please use caution.)

Doctors, hospitals, and pharmacies all charge different rates; you can keep costs down by comparison shopping. Higher medical costs don't always mean better care. To get the best care, you need to exercise your right to relevant, current, and understandable information about your case. If you learn about the proper medication and care for your problem, you can spot errors and even save your own life.

Hospital bills can be mind-boggling, but you can keep costs down by double-checking for accuracy. Because the average hospital stay costs thousands of dollars, it helps to tell the doctor that you want to approve and record every significant procedure performed during your stay. Once you're in the hospital, it helps to keep a log. A log can help to turn up a variety of clerical errors, such as billing twice for the same procedure or listing medications inaccurately. If the charges for drugs or other supplies are not given, you can ask for a detailed record. Insist that the hospital itemize each charge. When the bill comes and you find a charge you didn't approve, you can challenge the charge and refuse to pay it until you get an adequate explanation.

Creating Well-Being

More doctors and patients today are beginning to understand that stress either causes or aggravates many of our illnesses, or that the illness itself causes stress. Yet often it's not what happens to us that causes stress, but our perception of what happens to us.

Take, for example, the famous football player who had everything—money, fame, and good looks. During one game he was so badly injured he had to be carried off the field on a stretcher. Now, I know what I'd be thinking if I were that man.

I'd be thinking, "Oh, the pain . . . Oh, my career . . . Oh, the money . . . "

Instead, he turned to his stretcher bearers and said, "My mother was so right. I'm so glad I have on clean underwear."

His attitude created his response to his injury.

In our hearts, most of us realize we often make ourselves sick. Some people who are exposed to a communicable illness get sick, while others exposed to the same cause don't get sick. Psychological factors play a significant role.

Lately, even professionals are taking a closer look at what creates well-being. Research shows that connectedness—being loved, giving love, and being part of a caring family—has a real effect on wellness. The lack of such connections is associated with a higher mortality rate, arthritis, more hypertension, depression, coronary artery disease, and a diminished immune function.

A loving, supporting, multigenerational family structure promotes health. When things get stressful or difficult, caring families are life savers. This connectedness, belonging, or feeling of being loved can often override other risk factors. Ask any doctor if he or she makes patients well and you'll hear some downright humble replies.

Total health involves a state of well-being, or the ability to be at peace with ourselves. These feelings involve much more than our physical selves. Our physical, mental, social, and spiritual selves can combine to create a sense of inner joy.

We feel in control of our lives when we react positively even to difficult situations. Stress-resilient people have learned to find meaning in whatever they are doing right now. They enjoy learning and growing and have a clear vision of their own potential and the potential of others. They relish the diversity of people around them, have positive expectations, and a sense of hope. Stress-resilient people live creatively. They give attention and love to what matters most.

The happiest and healthiest people are those with the most positive thoughts; a positive mental attitude is more important to our health than medical advances. When we are emotionally well we feel connected to ourselves, family, friends, and human beings everywhere. When we are spiritually well, we live with a sense of meaning and purpose. We are able to give of ourselves for a purpose larger than ourselves.

People who are spiritually well feel a sense of mission and look at difficulties as opportunities for growth. They are able to find meaning and wisdom in the common, everyday difficulties and experiences of life. The depth of our gratitude for life and what it has to offer is the single most effective way to measure how well we are.

SAVING MONEY ON NONFOOD HOUSEHOLD EXPENSES

Children expose parents to strange maladies. Toilet tissue phobias, toothpaste testiness, peanut butter peritonitis, and soft-soap sacrifices are among the strange diseases that afflict childhood behavior patterns. Parents walk around scratching their heads, wondering where all the household supplies go.

Some days ago when I walked by the bathroom, I noticed one of my children wrapping the Charmin around her fist until it looked as if she were wearing a quilted, floral, pink boxing glove.

"Do you really think you need quite that much?" I asked my child (who will remain anonymous because someday she may grow up, learn how to read, find this book, and sue me). "I think five or six squares will do the job just fine."

When I walked into the kitchen, it looked as if the children had decided to redecorate with peanut butter. When my husband got home from work, I described the way our children wash their hands.

"First, they position one hand under the soft-soap dispenser, then they take the other hand, form a fist, and bring it down on the pump like a jackhammer, ramming out enough soap to fill the bottom of the sink," I said.

All these experiences brought back a flood of rather strange memories. After twenty years of lugging in case after case of personal hygiene supplies for his eight daughters, my father finally called an official family meeting. Dad sat at the head of the dining room table with a roll of toilet paper raised in the palm of his hand. I remember thinking he resembled the Statue of Liberty.

"Now that we are all assembled, I have something important to discuss," my father said with the straightest poker face I'd ever seen. "I will now demonstrate the proper way to use this common household product."

Dad unrolled one square, folded it twice, then began one of the most memorable lectures of my childhood.

The other night I heard my husband calling our children into the kitchen. I followed, stood in the doorway, and observed. My husband had a tube of toothpaste, a jar of peanut butter, a roll of toilet paper, and a container of soft soap lined in a neat row on the kitchen counter directly in front of him.

"I will now demonstrate the *incorrect* way to use each of these common household products," my husband began, ignoring the laughter-repressed faces of his eight children.

He then squeezed toothpaste over the toothbrush bristles and across the counter top in one mammoth glob. Grabbing the kitchen knife like a mass murderer, my husband slashed and smeared peanut butter down the side of the jar, across the counter, and onto the floor. Then he stepped in the mess and tracked the brown stuff over to the refrigerator door. Next, he left a peanut butter handprint on a gallon of milk that he slopped back to the counter top. He wiped his hands on a clean towel and threw it on the floor. Next, he wrapped a roll of toilet paper around his hand 287 times. Finally, he took his padded fist and rammed it down on the soft-soap dispenser until a huge, oozing blob dripped through his other hand and down into the sink.

"Now I will demonstrate the proper way to use these products," my husband added, but the children weren't listening. They were laughing so hard tears were spurting out their nostrils.

"I think I've seen this demonstration before," I said to my husband. "About thirty-two years ago. You do it much better than my father."

Parents through the ages have been known to give strange lectures and dining room demonstrations, all in the name of conserving the available cash on hand. After we pay our monthly bills we're usually unpleasantly surprised by how little is left for day-to-day expenses.

All families spend money on nonfood household expenses, so it helps to keep an eye out for good deals. For instance, there is always a best time of year to buy almost any product or service. Also, there is often a wide variation in prices between an item and its equivalent and between one retailer and another. So it pays to shop around for the best buy.

Family members can develop skills in *producing or repairing household items.* For instance, you can make or repair your own clothing or furniture. You can also perform many *services* you normally pay someone else for. I cut hair for my family because it saves us lots of money. By the time my children are old enough to realize I really don't know what I'm doing, they're teenagers and old enough to get a job and pay for their own haircuts.

Some parents give *lessons* to their own children, with varying degrees of success. For example, home music lessons work well for some families and away from home fishing lessons work well in others.

You can make many of your own *cleaning supplies.* (Safe substitutes for household products are listed in Appendix C.)

Personal hygiene products don't need to be expensive to work. Consumer publications consistently tell us that expensive cosmetics, soaps, lotions, and shampoos usually aren't any better than their cheaper alternatives, and sometimes they're worse. We have a family policy that we don't waste dollars on products that have an "image" unless we consciously decide we want to pay for it. I like cosmetic warehouse stores that sell discounted and discontinued products.

Sewing skills save money if you're paying attention. Cloth, just like ready-made clothing, makes a seasonal appearance and then goes out of date or style. If you buy sewing supplies from stores that carry last year's patterns and styles, you save. Just like ready-made clothing, fabrics can also be purchased as seconds. Irregularities that cause a cloth to be sold as a second include holes, shading problems, or loose threads. I recently made window toppers from beautiful, $40-a-yard upholstery material that sold at $2 a yard because it happened to have large holes in the fabric; I was able to easily cut around the holes. Items like old, out-of-style chair cushions and bedding fashions can be recovered with new sheets. Large clothing can be cut down to a smaller size and reused for a younger child.

Furniture and carpeting can take a big bite out of the family budget. Genuine sales in carpet are fairly rare, since styles don't change radically and there is no particular season for buying. We've found our best deals in shops that sell carpet seconds and irregulars. Most stores that sell seconds in floor covering aren't much to look at—they seldom have elevator music and chandeliers—but you can buy top-quality floor covering for a fraction of the retail price.

When you're in the market for furniture, it helps to let friends and relatives know, because most people have furniture gathering dust in the attic or out in the garage that they'd be glad to get rid of. Secondhand shops are also good places for furniture that needs a little fixing up.

You can also pick up serviceable furniture for next to nothing in used furniture stores and junk shops. We've found our best buys in secondhand furniture from garage sales and from newspaper want ads. Auction houses are another way to find good quality used furniture.

New furniture is one item that is most economically bought by sticking to top quality. We pay more initially for quality merchandise, but the long service we can expect from it makes the higher price worthwhile. Furniture with good prices and quality can be found in well-established, reputable furniture and department stores *if* they are having their seasonal clearance sales. Because markups on furniture are relatively high and furniture generally sells slowly, it's often possible to dicker the salesman down to a lower price even in the best stores.

With a little parental help, most children can rediscover frugal summer fun. *Vacations* don't have to set us back financially. Camping can cut transportation costs, keep food bills modest, and almost eliminate the cost of shelter. Purchasing camping equipment makes sense if you're going to use it over and over through a number of seasons. For those who plan to camp only once or twice a year, it makes more sense to borrow equipment from friends or family, or to rent it from stores or rental shops.

Swapping houses is another way to save on vacation costs. Lodging is free and meals can be made on site. The best way to find a house to swap is to write to a distant relative or friend and ask if they would like to vacation where you live. Some extended families like to pool their resources and build, buy, rent, or lease a vacation home. Many companies or organizations provide a vacation cabin or home for their employees.

Lodging prices at most hotels are negotiable. It never hurts to ask. Some hotels offer free breakfasts or free rides to airports and destinations. Some hotel and motel chains offer packages to attract families, so it pays to find a hotel that lets kids stay free in their parents' room or for half price in an adjoining room. Some hotels offer discounted meals for children, all-inclusive recreational programs for parents and kids, and packages that include free or reduced admission to nearby attractions.

Gifts are another expected but unplanned household expense. I like to buy unisex birthday presents by the dozen when I find a bargain on an item I know all children will enjoy. Then I wrap them and store them for my children to use for their friend's birthday parties. I write birthday and special occasion letters instead of making long-distance phone calls. Some families make birthdays and Christmas budgets affordable by making all their gifts by hand. Other families give time by spending the entire day doing anything the birthday child wants to do that doesn't cost money.

A *college education* is another difficult expense for families. In our family we try to match any money the children earn and put into a savings account for their college education. We encourage them to do well in school so they can compete for scholarship funds, and we try to set an example of the importance of education by continuing to acquire our own. Many parents feel responsible for their child's entire educational expenses after high school. Others expect the child to pay his or her own way. Some parents provide a combination of both. Students who are required to work for their education usually take their studies more seriously and appreciate the opportunity more than those who have parents who foot the entire bill.

The best way to start paying less on any nonfood household expense is to ask ourselves every time we fork over our hard-earned cash, "Could I provide this service or make this product for myself and save money?" or "Could I exchange a service or product I possess for a service or product I would like to have?"

When we change our minds enough to believe we can get by on less, we can. Sometimes less is more. We save ourselves a lot of headaches when we make the best use of what we have. If we can train our children to become Bargain Betty and Ben, we won't be required to give as many dining room table demonstrations on the proper use of toothpaste, toilet tissue, and peanut butter.

SAVING MONEY ON CLOTHING

I told my husband he should be eternally grateful he has a wife who doesn't often use a credit card. Why don't I use a credit card? Because I'm too tired to leave the house by the time I get all the kids ready to go. If, miracle of miracles, I happen to actually arrive at a store, the kids pick a fight, and my toddler gets lost . . . again.

It does something to a mother's sense of competence when she counts heads and finds seven when there should be eight after she hears the mall loudspeaker say, "There's a pathetic little lost girl wearing pink striped shorts screaming 'Mommy, come back! Mommy, come back!' in the elevator. You can pick up your neglected child at the incompetent parents' group session going on now in the department store basement, right next to the reject merchandise."

I realize I just need a sense of humor to handle family clothing shopping stress, but I can't find anything to laugh about.

At times like these, I try to remember that clothes are, after all, protection from the elements. Clothes were invented to keep us warm and comfortable. I don't believe we should go along with our society's feeling that the kind of clothes we wear will make us better looking or more popular, nor that we need to buy our clothing to impress our friends. Clothing consciousness has gotten just a tad out of hand when people start wearing designer labels on the *outside* of their clothes.

So what do you do to survive this clothing shopping stress? For starters, you can quit buying clothes, at least for a while. If you put your mind to it, I'll bet you can actually get by on the clothes you already have, at least for a few days. When we put a hold on clothing shopping for a certain period, it's amazing how resourceful we can be.

It usually takes years to acquire clothing shopping savvy. The family wardrobe is an expense most easily managed by planning ahead, a season at a time, so that you can get what you need for less money or get better clothes for the same money. If you wait to shop until you need something, you'll have to pay the peak-of-the-season price, and that's always higher.

It pays to shop in unusual places like secondhand and discount stores and to take advantage of extended family and friends who have good used clothing they want to get rid of. You can organize clothes-swapping organizations with your family, friends, or church units.

The trick of saving money by sewing your own clothes at home is in knowing when to bother. If you realistically figure the costs and find you save money and love to sew, it may be worth it; but if you usually lose money and hate sewing, it's not worth it. If you're good at it, making prom dresses or suits can save hundreds of dollars. If you're not good at it, making prom dresses or suits can cost hundreds of dollars because nobody will wear them. I've found that sewing window treatments, re-covering chair cushions, and cutting and hemming worn pants into shorts are some of the easiest ways to save money by sewing.

Young children grow so quickly that buying expensive, trendy clothes for tots and active grade-school children is a huge waste of money. I am a great fan of thrift shops such as Deseret Industries. I donate any clothing we don't need and buy what we do need. When I spend only a few dollars for my children's clothes, I don't have to waste time worrying about holes and stains. Deseret Industries also washes and sanitizes everything they sell, so I have the added advantage of knowing what an article of clothing looks like after it's been washed.

There is an art to secondhand clothing shopping. You have to be willing to spend additional time sorting through outdated or worn pieces to find good quality used clothing. It helps to walk through the local mall and study the clothing displays for ideas on up-to-date looks you can duplicate at thrift-store prices. Classic cuts and neutral colors are always in style. Many articles of clothing are mis-sized or mislabeled—so check all departments. Leave the tags on clothing you may need to return.

Many parents dress their young children to suit the parents' taste and show off the family income level. This is dumb. Young children should be allowed to wear inexpensive clothing they can soil and destroy as they work at the difficult task of growing up.

If my child is still in diapers, I like clothes that are easy to take off and put back on for quick diaper changes. If my child is an active preschooler or grade schooler, I find sturdy, comfortable clothes that protect knees and allow for comfort before looks and style. I buy only wash and wear. If my children are in junior high or high school and demand more expensive, trendy clothes, they are old enough to earn the money to buy their own clothes. It saves me time and money to buy white socks, sheets, and towels. Everything matches and stains can be bleached out.

As a former seamstress and inspector for a clothing manufacturer, I have also learned to take a good look before I buy. In my job as a clothing inspector, I learned that any piece of clothing can be inspected easily and closely in only a few seconds. Look for wide, reinforced side seams and hems, matching patterns or plaids, details such as snaps, hooks, covered buttons, or extra buttons, reinforced collars, and lining. Before I buy, I like to turn the garment inside out and decide if it will last through multiple washings.

A few dry-clean-only clothes in a wardrobe are plenty. The real money savers are clothes that can be washed at home. Also, it pays not to buy anything unless you can wear it with at least two items of clothing you already have. What good is an article of clothing, even if it's on sale, if you don't have anything to wear it with? Neutral shades like white, beige, blue, or black can be worn with almost anything.

If you shop with a friend or family member, it's often easy to buy something because *they* like it and not because *you* like it. Even overbearing salespeople can talk many of us into purchases if we're not careful.

I used to think the word *sale* meant getting a bargain, but I have since learned that some sales are legitimate and some are not. Some sales are simply a way of getting rid of cheap, outdated, or discontinued merchandise. It isn't a good buy if it's junk, not at any price. Also, it isn't a good buy if you don't need it.

For the best selection, shop in February and March for spring clothes and in August and September for fall clothes. Even better, if you can wait, is to buy clothes after the season has passed. Buy winter clothing on clearance in the spring. Buy spring clothing on clearance in the fall.

Sometimes boys' or men's departments carry jeans, shirts, or jackets for much less than the children's or women's department. Men's and boys' clothing is often made to last longer, too. Large sizes in the children's or teen department often offer women with small builds the same styles for less money.

There are a growing number of factory outlet stores that sell seconds and surplus clothing. A flawed garment, no matter how minor the flaw, cannot be sold for the full retail price, even if the flaw is not detectable to the average eye, so these outlet or discount stores often offer good quality for about half the price.

Finally, for motivation to save on clothing purchases, think back to the last shopping trip with children!

And now, just for fun, I'd like to give you a few very important rules all moms and dads should know before they tread into the stores with their wild, untamed children.

Rule #1: Never take the children with you when you go school shopping.

If you take the children along, they will yell embarrassing insults at their siblings, have to go to the bathroom seventeen times in three minutes, hate everything in the store that is affordable, love everything in the store that is too expensive, and make the shoe salesman pass out for want of fresh air.

Rule #2: Always take the children with you when you go school shopping.

The only way to be absolutely sure your child will absolutely hate an article of clothing and refuse to wear it is to pick it out yourself. Children have their own set of rules and one of them reads, "If mom or dad thinks an article of clothing is fashionable, run for your life. You'll soon be the laughingstock of the high school."

Rule #3: Always buy leather shoes.

Leather shoes allow the child's foot to breathe in comfort.

Leather stretches to conform to the shape of the child's foot. Leather is better than plastic. Leather is expensive.

Rule #4: Never buy leather shoes.

You can't wipe off leather shoes or throw them into the washing machine after they've been through a recess on a wet, muddy field. Plastic may not breathe, but it takes a licking and keeps on ticking.

Rule #5: Buy clothing to fit.

Children should wear comfortable clothing that fits. If you buy clothing and shoes the child will grow into, the child will suddenly stop growing for two years and seven months.

Rule #6: Buy clothing two sizes too big.

Every parent knows that children suddenly grow two inches immediately after you've been school shopping. If the child complains because the shoes won't stay on his feet, his pants drag, and his shirt falls off his shoulders, tell him to hurry up and grow, for goodness sake.

Rule #7: Always buy quality.

Good quality shoes and clothing last longer and save you money in the long run.

Rule #8: Never buy quality.

Children rip $50 jeans just as fast as they rip $7 factory outlet brands.

Rule #9: Carefully watch your children at all times so that they will not wander off and become lost while you are busy shopping.

Careless parents shouldn't be allowed out in public with their poor, unfortunate children.

Rule #10: Carefully watch your children at all times so that you will know when you should wander off and become lost.

When your children begin a contest to see who can belch the loudest in Mervyn's department store, pretend you don't know them, wander off, and get lost.

Following these rules may not make your shopping adventure

smooth and carefree, but I guarantee they will keep you totally confused and misguided.

SAVING MONEY ON TRANSPORTATION

One of the biggest roadblocks to debt-free living for the average family is the purchase of a newer, fancier car than you need.
Cars are not a good value for the money. Many of us buy cars to
show off and get attention. If we want to get attention or show off,
we don't have to buy an expensive new car—we can stuff peacock
feathers down our pant legs and pump our arms up and down.
We'd get a lot more attention and we'd be money ahead.

The best way to save money on cars is not to own one. If walking is not an option, you can do the next best thing: drive an old
car. If you drive two cars, you can consider selling one. The point
is, the less money we sink into our cars, the better off we'll be.

The last time my husband and I bought a car, our teenage
daughter totaled it a few weeks later. About a month later, our other
teenage daughter wrecked our other car. Luckily both of our children were all right. Lesson learned: don't get emotionally attached
to cars. Emotional attachments to children are permitted.

The next time we buy a car I'm going to drive it home, take out
a hammer, and put a dent in the right fender; that way I won't have
to worry about how long it's going to take for this one to get
wrecked. We ought to sign a new bill into law that prohibits all
driver's license holders from traveling at speeds greater than their
age. Hence, a sixteen-year-old can go sixteen miles per hour.

If you absolutely have to buy a car, then it's important to
remind yourself that a car is not a reflection of your success, personality, or self-worth. A car is not a legitimate way to boost your
ego. A car is a swirling black vacuum that sucks up your money. It
will not make any of us instantly popular to drive an expensive car—
except with the car dealer. If car dealers smile when they see you
coming, you know you have a problem.

A car is . . . transportation. A car takes us from point A to point

B. The kind of car we drive will not make us more popular unless our friends are trying to butter us up so they can borrow our car. I drive one of those nine-passenger, saggy-rear-end station wagons that were popular about twenty-seven years ago. No one ever butters me up to borrow my car, not even my teenagers. This old wagon has a number of scratches and a few rust spots I like to refer to as medals of honor for a car that has survived World War III. I drive my family of ten around, packed in like sardines. When we go over bumps, I ask the kids in the rear to raise theirs. I never worry about someone scratching the car in the parking lot, and hey, if someone steals it, who cares? The thief will have to come up with the repair costs.

The truth is, the cost of owning and operating a motor vehicle is a nightmare if we consider payments, interest, depreciation, insurance, taxes, gasoline, oil, maintenance, repair, tires, parking and tolls, license fees, registration, and all the other stuff that comes with car ownership. The average annual cost of owning and operating a vehicle eats up a major portion of our disposable income.

The initial price of the car is just the beginning. Insuring the car is the never-ending story. Insurance rates for the same coverage can vary by hundreds of dollars, so it pays to take time to shop around. Ask friends, check the yellow pages, call the state insurance department, check consumer guides, call insurance companies and agents. This will give you an idea of price ranges and tell you which companies or agents have the lowest prices.

The insurer you select should offer both fair prices *and* great service. It's smart to talk to a number of insurers and get a feeling for the quality of their service and ask them what they would do to lower our costs. You can check the company's financial rating and get price quotes.

To lower the rate, ask for the highest deductibles you can afford and consider dropping expensive comprehensive and collision insurance after the car gets old. The purpose of insurance is to protect against big losses, not against the things you can afford to pay on your own. The deductible, of course, is the amount of money you pay before you make a claim. By requesting higher deductibles on collision and comprehensive (fire and theft) coverage, you can lower your costs substantially. The blue book, available at dealers and banks, can tell you how much the car is worth.

Also, if you have adequate health insurance, you may be paying for duplicate medical coverage in your auto policy. In some states, eliminating this coverage could lower your personal injury protection cost by up to 40 percent.

Before you buy a new or used car, it makes sense to check into insurance costs. Cars that are expensive to repair, or that are favorite targets for thieves, have much higher insurance premiums. Costs tend to be lowest in rural communities and highest in central cities where there is more traffic congestion.

Some companies offer discounts to motorists who drive fewer than a predetermined number of miles a year. Others offer discounts for automatic seat belts or air bags. Some insurers offer discounts for more than one car, no accidents in three years, driver over fifty years of age, driver training courses, anti-theft devices, anti-lock brakes, and good grades for students.

It doesn't make financial sense to buy a new car—they simply depreciate in value too quickly. A good used car is always a better deal. Before looking at used cars, it helps to evaluate your family needs in terms of size, body style, and how much money you're willing to spend.

When buying a car from an individual, it's better to deal with someone you know, because friends are less likely to lie about why they are selling the car. As a general rule, people don't sell cars that are running well, so that's the risk you take when you buy a used car. It helps to be cautious. Rental-car companies sell late-model cars that are generally well maintained and driven primarily on the highway. Car dealers can also be a good source, but you usually have to pay more. Choose someone who has a good reputation and who has been in business for several years. You can contact the Better

Business Bureau to find out about complaints against the dealer. If possible, get the name of the previous owner of the car and talk to him or her.

The U.S. Customs Service sells seized automobiles, and the U.S. General Services Agency sells surplus property. Other sources include the IRS, the Department of Defense, and local financial institutions and police departments. When considering a used car, it helps to check *Consumer Reports'* annual "Buying Guide Issue" and other such sources.

Mechanical misfit alert: You don't have to be an expert to check out a few key areas on any used car you're considering buying. According to my mechanic, even motor morons like me can quickly evaluate a few things before we fork over a few dollars to have a professional check the car.

Cars that sag on one side, tires that bulge, frayed brake pedals, and lights that don't work are not good signs. There should not be globs of oil or rust floating on top of the water in the radiator or puffs of blue smoke billowing from the tailpipe. Oil leakage under the car could also spell trouble. According to my mechanic, test driving a car is mostly a matter of listening for weird noises. Clanging and thumping noises, along with engine parts falling beneath the car when moving, are serious reasons to reconsider the purchase. Screeching noises indicate you were foolish enough to take your children along for the test drive.

After you've checked out a few items for yourself, it's wise to have a trusted mechanic check out the car and tell you about any problems he or she can spot. Mechanical problems don't need to prevent you from buying a car, but you should know how much it will cost to repair them and figure that in as you consider the purchase price.

As you consider the price, it's important to check the car's "blue book" value, or the average trade-in and retail price of the car. These are listed in the *National Automobile Dealers Association's Official Used Car Guide,* which you can find in the reference section of a library or at almost any financial institution. You usually don't want to pay the full retail price.

If you hope to negotiate a good price, you need to be prepared to walk away from the deal even if you fall in love with the car. And remember that the purchase price is only one of several factors to consider. Depreciation, gas mileage, repair costs, and insurance rates should also affect the cost.

Once you buy a car, it pays to take good care of it. You really should read the owner's manual, change the oil every three months or three thousand miles, have hoses and belts replaced regularly, and rotate the tires at recommended intervals.

After you become the proud owner of a car or truck, it's also important to move onward and upward to a higher level of understanding about the way vehicles and families mix. There are three different periods of car-need-ness in families, known as
—before the children can drive,
—after the children can drive, and
—after the children leave home.

Each period requires a different strategy from parents.

Before your children are old enough to drive, you don't need to worry about much except how to keep your kids from murdering each other in the backseat. Our personal search has always been for a car to match the number of seat belts and window seats we needed in our ever-expanding family. We also looked for interior upholstery that would hide child bomb stains. After we had children old enough to drive, the search was on for a good stress therapist.

Driving a nice new car with expensive collision insurance doesn't always make sense, mainly because we can't afford it and still have enough money left for food. Sometimes we're forced to choose between having our teen buy his or her own insurance or scaling down to a used, inexpensive car with no-fault insurance. There is a reason why teens raise our insurance rates. It's called reality.

After all the children are raised, you get your turn to buy the car you've always wanted. You now become a distinguished member of the driving community everyone enjoys honking at because you drive under the speed limit and hog the passing lane.

It's amazing how quickly our attitudes toward cars and driving change as we change perspective from child to parent. When my sixteen-year-old daughter presented her application for a driver's license the other day, I asked the lady at the desk if she had a class for parents of teenage drivers. The lady just smiled.

While I was waiting for my daughter to have her picture taken, I remembered my own mother's feet braced against the dashboard on my maiden voyage as a driver. I was determined to pass this mothering test of nerves with a little more finesse. The problem was, I happened to remember that only a few years earlier this daughter had ridden her bicycle into a pine tree because . . . "Oh, Mom, I forgot how to make it stop!"

The real testing came later when my daughter asked if she could drive me home. Parenting books don't warn us about the Dr. Jekyll and Mr. Hyde transformation that takes place in a parent's body when he or she moves into the car's passenger seat and the teenager moves behind the wheel.

One minute I was trying to act cool, calm, and comatose and the next I was bracing my feet on the floorboard, gripping the door handle, and uttering strange sentences like:

"Oh . . . Oh! Didn't you see that car?"

"Turn here. No! Not *right* here! Up there, where there's a road to turn on!"

"You're doing fine, dear. No. I'm not nervous. I always sit like this."

When older parents tried to warn me years ago about the perils of parenting adolescents, I always spouted back, "Look, if a child can go to the bathroom all by himself, he can't be all bad. Count your blessings."

Then came THE CALL. "Mom," April said with a shaking voice. "I've been in a car accident."

At that moment, I began to understand what those older, wiser parents had tried to tell me. I tend to get excessively excited when one of my children learns how to walk or talk. I need the same enthusiasm when one of my children learns to drive away without me—and comes back whole and healthy.

No matter how many wet towels, smelly socks, grade reports, elections, and proms I've been through with my teens, it all melts in a life-and-death situation where a single seat belt is all that comes between my child and death. There is an awesome magic and terror in watching our children transform into adults right before our clenched teeth and white knuckles.

No, family transportation just isn't what it used to be, especially when we move over to the passenger side.

SAVING MONEY ON HOUSING

We don't have to have a big fancy house or condo to be absolutely terrific people. The type of house we live in will not make us happy, healthy, or wise. Our house or apartment keeps the rain off, gives us a place to get warm, and affords a little privacy. The less protection and privacy we need, the less house we need. My husband spent several years in Samoa where only stupid people who loved getting heat strokes had solid walls in their houses.

In affluent societies, many of us buy a house the same way we buy a new car or fancy clothes—for show. We want our friends, family members, and strangers to notice, admire, and respect us. In truth, the thing that attracts people to a house is not the brickwork, but the people who live there.

Some of our best memories are made in the most humble living arrangements with the most meager resources. When my husband and I married, all our friends lived in cozy two-bedroom apartments. We lived in the rear of a hundred-year-old former hotel. A beauty parlor occupied the space on the other side of our kitchen wall; a real estate office, the other side of our living room wall; and a loan office, the other side of our bedroom wall. In the apartment above us, a man and wife used to get drunk and beat each other up.

I had to wait until after business hours if I wanted to sing in the shower. The apartment had to be fumigated for cockroaches before we moved in. We had no windows or bathtub, and my bathroom sink was attached to our living room wall. I used to tape landscapes to the wall above my kitchen sink and pretend I could see out.

If I tried to wash dishes or clothes during business hours, the operator of the beauty parlor would scream at me because she didn't have enough hot water for her customers. We lived on the corner of Center and Main streets, and if I stepped outside too quickly, I put myself in danger of being run over by busy traffic. The traffic light on the corner lit up our bedroom with alternating red, green, and yellow lights.

That place was all we could afford at the time, since we felt I should stay home and take care of our babies while my husband went to school and worked full time. Talk about a memory maker. That apartment was also the greatest attitude adjuster I've ever had, because it has transformed every other place we've lived into a dream home.

Not unlike childbirth stories, young married living arrangements tend to get worse with each telling. Certainly they give us a better appreciation for everything that comes later. When I finally moved into my first new home, I walked around the rooms in a state of awe every morning, opening each window one by one. Housing doesn't have to be first rate to offer some first-rate memories.

Where we live is probably the biggest financial decision we'll ever make (except for choice of occupation). If we spend too much or too little on our housing, it's possible to put a huge dent in life quality. Even though housing generally takes the biggest bite from our budgets, it's easy to ignore sound decision making. Housing decisions have to be made with our *hearts* and our *heads*.

For instance, the decision between renting or owning boils down to a lifestyle choice as well as a financial choice. Any analysis of buying a home solely on financial grounds is going to fall short, because the value of home ownership cannot be found in money alone. Neighborhood pride, living space control, privacy, equity, and building up a community are advantages that mean a great deal to some people. Renting, on the other hand, offers the advantage of fixed payments for housing, no accountability for breakdowns and repairs, and freedom from yard work.

My husband was a real estate salesman for several years, and I observed the buying habits of many of his clients. I discovered that most people buy houses in much the same way they buy cheese puffs—on impulse. This is dumb. For example, one couple bought a hundred-year-old house because they fell in love with the fireplace mantel. These people had no idea how much work goes in to fixing up an old house. They ended up hating the fireplace mantel, the house, and each other before they were through.

When you shop for a house, the best thing is *not* to start with the house. Better housing decisions are made when you take the time to look at yourself and your family first. A home should suit you—in design, cost, appearance, size, and type. It helps to take a good look at your living patterns, then decide what's important to you and your family and what is not.

For instance, if privacy is important, you need to look for a secluded location. If you like to party with family and friends, you should look for a home with a large kitchen and dining room. If your children lead separate lives, you need to look for a house with ample bedroom space that will keep them from disrupting each other. If you hate home repairs, you should look for a newer home.

Once you understand your needs, it's better to focus first on location, then later on the actual house. As you look for a good location, keep in mind how long it will take you to get to work and other places you frequently visit. It pays to become aware of zoning ordinances, building codes, local property tax ranges, and the availability and price of utilities. It's wise to pay attention to the neighbors, local schools, shopping areas, fire and police protection, libraries, parks, post office, banks, hospitals, churches, and services like water, sewage, and garbage collection.

The lot is another important location consideration. People who love yard work should look for big lots or yards, and people who hate yard work should look for small lots or plan to hire a gardener.

After you consider the location, the next important question to answer is affordability. When you talk to your realtor or banker about a mortgage, he'll tell you how much money you qualify to borrow, based on your income. These figures give you limited information, because you may or may not be able to afford a house in that price range. These figures give the lender and agent an idea of whether you are qualified to get a loan, but they don't really tell you if you can afford the house. These figures don't take into account the number of children you have, the stability of your income, the amount you give to charity, or the amount you regularly need to save. A good way to be house poor is to borrow right up to your credit limit.

Most experts say the purchase price should not exceed $2\frac{1}{2}$ times your annual income or that monthly payments should approximate weekly income. After you consider what the experts say, it's wise to sit back, be realistic, and try to settle on a reasonable amount that won't strap you. There are always unexpected expenses that come out of nowhere, but you don't have to penny-pinch either. You spend the most important moments of your life in your home, and it should be the best you can comfortably manage on your income.

In spite of what you've heard, there aren't really many bargains out there. The law of supply and demand works pretty well in relating price to value. If a buyer pays less initially, he'll most likely make up the difference through higher maintenance costs or declining resale price as the house ages.

Because houses wear out, looking for a new home and looking for an older home require two different strategies. There is not as much room to bargain on the price of a new home as there is on an older home. Quality of material and workmanship are important to a new home. How well these materials have stood the test of time is important when considering an older home. When the IRS gives landlords of rented houses a depreciation allowance, it is based on the assumption that a building will wear out in forty years.

It's important to find out about the person from whom you will be buying the house. Do all you can to make sure the seller has not misrepresented the condition of the house. Be sure to obtain clear title to the property. When selling a home you can cut realtor costs by negotiating for a lower commission, using a discount broker, or selling the home on your own.

Before hiring a builder, it's wise to check with the local office of the National Association of Home Builders and the Better Business Bureau to see if they have had any complaints. Ask the builder the name of his or her bank; then visit the bank and talk with one of the commercial officers about the builder. Ask the builder for his or her business number and home number. Ask the builder for the names of a few people he has built houses for; then call and see what they think of the quality of his work.

Most of this home-buying business will finish up with a mortgage. A mortgage is money we borrow, then hand over to buy property; at the same time, the property becomes security for the loan, which we pay off over a long period of time, with interest, in regular installments. Obtaining the mortgage and buying the property are two separate transactions, even though both take place at the same time at a single sitting, called a closing. At the closing you receive title to the property—that is, you become the actual owner—with all of an owner's legal rights *and* obligations. If you fail to repay the loan, the lender can take possession of the property and foreclose or sell the house to repay the debt. The lender has a lien on the property until it's paid for. A lien is a creditor's legal claim on a property for the satisfaction of a debt.

On a brighter note, mortgages are usually the least expensive loans, and the interest is tax deductible. While the interest rate on mortgages is comparatively low, the total dollar amount of interest we pay on a home mortgage is humongous. Most homeowners pay two or three times more in interest than the house sold for in the first place.

If you don't plan to keep the house until the mortgage is paid off, it's a good idea to figure out the costs and benefits of the different kinds of mortgages over the period of time you plan to stay there. When you take the time to come up with solid facts and figures, you can make a wiser decision on which mortgage is right for you and your family. The longer you plan to stay in the house, the more valuable the shorter mortgage.

Adjustable-rate loans are right for some people. With these loans, the rate fluctuates according to the interest available at any given time. Any increase is usually limited to 2 percentage points a year and 5 to 6 percentage points over the life of the loan. If you are going to stay in the home for only two or three years, an adjustable-rate loan might be right. Fixed-rate mortgages are usually better for people who expect to remain in their homes for five years or more. If rates plunge, you can refinance. If rates go up, you're locked in at a good rate.

The biggest eye-opener of my life was a glance at the amortization schedule for our home mortgage. That's when I realized we would pay for our home three times over before our mortgage was paid off. That one brief visit with my amortization schedule was all it took to convince me that paying off the mortgage early was a great goal.

One simple way to pay off a mortgage sooner than expected is by refinancing when interest rates go down and changing from a thirty-year fixed rate to a twenty- or fifteen-year payment schedule. In refinancing, lenders often charge two to three points for a new loan. A point equals 1 percent of the loan amount. For example, three points on a $100,000 mortgage loan would add $3,000 to the refinancing charges. To find out roughly how long it will take to break even, divide closing costs by the amount saved each month.

Other ways to pay off a mortgage early are to make one extra principal payment each year, pay every two weeks instead of twice a month, or apply all the second wage-earner's income toward the house loan until the loan balance is paid off. Some people use tax-free retirement funds to pay off their mortgage, while others ask their parents to give them their inheritance early. Parents can give their children up to $10,000 per parent per year, tax free.

It's also tempting to borrow money against your home for consumer goods, adding a home-equity loan to the mortgage. People who sell the use of money know the secrets of enticing us to borrow more money. Money lenders often send us personal letters to remind us of all the wonderful things we could enjoy in our lives if we only had more money. But it doesn't make sense to borrow more money to do them, especially when your home is on the line.

Aside from all the financial talk about housing, our homes and apartments provide more than protection from the elements. They give us a place to make memories and a few rooms where we can learn to love those closest to us. The actual bricks and beams are not valuable. What happens inside those four walls is valuable and in the end will sum up the meaning of our lives. Money can buy a house, but it can't buy a home.

Our real challenge is to create a place where peaceful feelings can be felt and where love can grow. The other day I watched my young son slide into home base during a little league game.

The umpire shouted, "Safe!"

It occurred to me that in this troubled world, the greatest gift I can offer my children is a home. It would be nice if every mother, father, and child knew they were always "safe" at home.

If we really want our incomes to seem a little less gross, we need to quit trying to impress other people and wholeheartedly take on the challenge of simplifying our lives by reducing expenses on the necessities of life—food, health care, household expenses, clothing, transportation, and housing. In the end, we no longer have to get confused when experts talk to us about net or gross income, because we know grossless income will come when we remember this: All we earn is ours to save, keep, and give away.

CHAPTER 4

Work Is a Blessing, So Smile, Won't You?

That they should let no pride nor haughtiness disturb their peace; that every man should esteem his neighbor as himself; laboring with their own hands for their support.

—MOSIAH 27:4

POSSIBILITIES

Once there was a man who worked at an office. One day the man did not make his quota on widgets and gaggles, and he received a stern reprimand from his supervisor. The man was feeling very tired when he walked home that night.

When he walked past a ditch, the man noticed a long brown string floating in the water. Even though he was tired, the man bent down and picked the string out of the water.

As the man walked home he thought, "Oh, the things I could do with this string. Why, I could string beads on it and make a necklace for my wife. I could paint a lovely picture, then run the string through the fresh paint to make a wonderful wispy cloud design in the sky."

While the man was contemplating all the things he could do with his string, it started to rain. The man picked up two old pieces of cardboard on the side of the road, tied them together with the string, and made himself an umbrella to stay dry from the rain.

"Oh, the things I could do with this string," the man thought when the rain stopped and the sun came out. "I could write letters in the sand or tie the end of a braid with a bow. I could take my dog for a walk or make myself a new tie."

Just then a gust of wind came up and blew against the man.

"Oh, the things I could do with this string," the man thought. "I could attach it to a kite and let it soar high above me

99

for hours. I could tie up chimes on the roof and listen to their music. I could hang cookies from our trees for the birds to eat."

Just then the man noticed a sign on the road that said Welcome to Plain City, with an arrow pointing to the right.

"Oh, the things I could do with this string," the man thought. "I could tie a sign to our front door that says, Welcome to the Fine House of the Man with the Most Wonderful String."

Just then the man's shoelace broke. The man broke the string into two pieces, then bent down and tied the shorter string to the broken shoelace and fixed his shoe.

"Oh, the things I could do with this string," the man thought. "I could tie up the broken exhaust pipe on my car or loop my important keys to my belt loop. I could sew up that hole in my coat."

Just then the man heard a train and a jet plane pass by.

"Oh, the things I could do with this string," the man thought. "I could tie it to another piece of string and another, until I had the longest piece of string in the world. I could tie my long string to the end of rocket ships so pilots could trail messages back down to their mothers. I could throw my string out to rescue people drowning in the sea."

Just then the man saw a child run by.

"Oh, the things I could do with this string," the man thought. "I could tie the mittens to my children's coats so they wouldn't get lost. I could sew on missing buttons and tie up my daughter's pigtails and dreams."

Just then the man remembered he was probably late for supper, so he ran the rest of the way home.

When the man arrived at his front gate, his wife was sitting on the front step frowning.

"You're late," the man's wife said. "And what are you doing dragging that piece of dirty old string? Don't bring that dirty old string into my clean house."

The man looked down at his string. He hadn't noticed it

was dirty until now. After a long moment, the man took a deep breath, put the string in his pocket, and hitched up his pants. Then he threw out his arms and embraced his wife.

"Woman," the man said to his wife, "we have some important work to do. Let's go inside."

"Oh, the wonderful things I can do with my wife," the man thought as they walked through the door.

Before long all the man's children were hanging on the man's legs. He reached down and drew them close.

"Oh, the wonderful things I can do with my children," the man said.

Later that day the man pulled the string from his pocket and hung a sign on the front door that read, Welcome to the Fine House of the Man with the Most Wonderful Family. 🙩

THE DIVINE PLAN OF WORK

One evening, soon after my husband and I moved into our first new home, we seeded our front yard dirt with grass. The next morning, my husband told me it was important to keep the dirt wet or the grass seeds wouldn't sprout. Then he kissed me on the cheek and left for work.

Since it was the middle of a hot July, this wet dirt assignment was more than a full-time job. On top of that, I was pregnant and had two baby daughters to care for. I remember standing out on our front porch, feeling lightheaded and nauseated, squirting the dirt for hours while my one- and two-year-old daughters tumbled down the steps, threw their shoes in the ditch, and stuffed rocks up their noses. After days and days of constant watering, our front yard began growing the biggest, greenest weeds in the whole neighborhood.

"This is my life," I remember mumbling as I squirted the dirt. "All I do is water weeds. I feed one end of the girls and clean up the other. Nothing I do really matters. All I do is water weeds."

A few days later, I started having serious complications with my pregnancy; and late one night, I began hemorrhaging. My husband quickly called a neighbor to watch our children, then raced me to the emergency room of the nearest hospital. After the doctor arrived at the hospital and slowed the bleeding, he told us that our baby had died.

Leaving the hospital that night with empty arms was one of the hardest things I've ever done. When we arrived home, we found our two baby daughters asleep on our bed. Now, I'd always loved my daughters, but never quite like I did at that moment.

"Thank you, God," I whispered. "They are alive. It is such a miracle to have a child who is alive."

Several days later when I went out to check on our front lawn of weeds, I found something I hope I never forget. If I got down on my hands and knees and took out a magnifying glass, I could see tiny green blades of grass so small they looked like green sewing thread. My elderly neighbor walked over and told me that in time those tiny blades of grass would crowd out the weeds and we'd have a beautiful lawn; all my watering and weeding would pay off. I just had to have faith and patience in the growing season. She was right. In time, the grass crowded out the weeds and we did indeed have a beautiful lawn.

Our life is a growing season full of work and waiting with hope. Without the faith that all our work will eventually crowd out the weeds and bring a harvest, we miss something precious—we miss joy in the growing. To miss the joy in the growing is to miss it all.

Those beautiful baby daughters, whom I found asleep on my bed when I returned from the hospital that night, are now beautiful grown women. They no longer stumble down steps, throw their shoes in the ditch, and stuff rocks up their noses. Each day when I look into their eyes I am reminded that, in time, all my bumbling efforts will crowd out the weeds, that common, everyday tasks, if done with faith and joy, are what a meaningful life is all about.

The most miserable people I know are those who constantly try to avoid work or those who think someone else should pay their way. People who find joy in labor, no matter what the work is, are happier and healthier than those who dread work and view labor as a roadblock in their quest for idle hours.

Work is something we do for other people that ends up paying us back. Work is really the way we keep in step with the music of living things; the way we have to pay back our debt for the gift of life. When we're idle, we're no longer dancing with the change of seasons and the song of growth. All living things join together to make the music of the final score—the never-ending melody of life.

The work we do fulfills a divine purpose if it is done with love. To avoid labor is to lose step with the infinite plan. Work is not a curse. When we work, we begin to fulfill the measure, the hope, of our creation. When we choose to work with love, we choose to embrace life. If we fashion the work of our hands into the work of our hearts, all work is honorable.

Work, paid or unpaid, is absolutely necessary to our happiness. Yet our life's work doesn't have to draw a sweat to be meaningful. I know an elderly woman who is confined to her bed, but she is happy and feels needed because she has learned to redefine work in ways she is capable of performing. This woman sends out birthday cards to everyone in her neighborhood. When people visit her, they go away feeling uplifted by her positive attitude and gratitude for life. "My job is to cheer up people," this woman smiles.

Most of us would be happier if we broadened our definition of work. Work isn't just something we get paid for or something we do eight hours a day far from home. We can perform paid or unpaid work outside the home or paid or unpaid work inside the home. Work can be a financial and spiritual solution to many of our pressing problems.

HOME-BASED WORK WITHOUT PAY

The other afternoon my daughter walked into the study and asked me for a ride into town. At the time, I was trying to work on a new book and my two-year-old had just tumbled into the room sobbing because her Barbie doll had suffered an unexpected decapitation.

"Mom, I need a ride . . . *NOW!*" my teenager insisted.

I'd spent most of the afternoon sewing silver arrow points on my eight-year-old's Cub Scout shirt, preparing to teach my college writing class later that evening, running up and down stairs between several batches of laundry, toilet training an eager but mostly unsuccessful toddler, fixing a meal for a friend who was caring for her dying mother, refereeing the latest sibling war, and cleaning up after several microwave murders.

"You should let me know beforehand when you need a ride. I have lots of important things to do," I answered, a little annoyed.

"Important? What do *you* do that's so important? All you do is stay home and clean up the house all day," my daughter said.

Her remark stung, but I understood her feeling. Like my daughter, when I was a girl I also placed little value on unpaid work. I'd rather work in my neighbor's orchard picking cherries and get paid than cook or wash dishes for nothing at home. When I was young, I believed people were paid for *important* work.

I've since learned that people are seldom financially rewarded for the most important and most lasting work they do. Though we receive financial payment for some of the work we perform, the most important work a man or woman will ever do is never paid for in dollars and cents.

I know many talented, bright people who choose to work at home or in their community instead of in the labor market—the feelings they receive from giving service are of far greater value to them than the money they could otherwise accumulate. The marketplace generally pays us for staying away from our inner selves, our families, and our friends. I get paid dollars for writing newspaper columns and family life books and for teaching composition classes. I don't get paid in dollars for sitting quietly in the chair reading a book to my two-year-old, reattaching Barbie's head, sewing on silver arrow points, fixing a meal for a friend—or, for that matter, giving my teenage daughter a ride to town. On the other hand, I am paid in ways greater than money when I give such service.

Because of the tension between work for money and work for emotional fulfillment, it is (and always will be) difficult to decide where, when, and why we work. It will always be tempting to trade the majority of our time for money. But it doesn't make sense to work for possessions that can never satisfy us. When it comes to possessions, we can never have enough. Many possessions are things we hoard for fear we'll need them someday. That feeling of fear or dread that we may not have enough someday is a thirst that can never be satisfied.

Whether we receive a paycheck or not, the work we do can be physical evidence of our love. The service we render in our own homes is the most important work we'll ever do. Creating a safe, loving environment where people can grow and reach their potential is no small matter. There is honor and deep sustaining value in the efforts of families who devote their time to each other and the larger family of man.

HOME-BASED WORK FOR PAY

It wasn't that many generations ago when families worked, played, and lived together. Home-based work sustained life. Today, most of us work outside our homes; but more and more of us are searching for ways to come back home physically, emotionally, and spiritually. Many couples and single parents are looking for ways to afford to stay home by changing where, when, and why they work. Most of us desire to create a home that is the race instead of the pit-stop, but for many of us the cost of living is making that dream increasingly difficult.

Home-based paid work is one solution to the financial concerns facing families today. A home business is not for everyone, but as the computer age makes it easier and easier to find work outside the office, it is becoming a workable solution for growing numbers of families.

I work at home. Along with cleaning, cooking, child care, and slave labor, I write newspaper columns, magazine articles, and books. I think it's a great way to combine paid work and raising a family, for the benefit of both. I love my family. I also love to write. Most of us love to work at what we love. My husband told me he probably wouldn't go to the bank every day if they quit paying him. I'm lucky. I do something I'd keep doing even if nobody paid me.

There are literally thousands of ways for stay-at-home parents to generate income if they retrain their minds to first focus on solving their neighbor's problems instead of their own. People *pay* to have their problems solved. When we solve a problem for someone else, we usually have our financial problems solved in the process.

I developed the following list in my own search for home-based, income-producing work possibilities. These are services and occupations that can make a real difference to your family finances.

Abstracting and Indexing Service. Abstracting and indexing services usually include book indexing, computer database indexing, and abstracting for in-house corporate use. Abstracting consists of reading articles or books and condensing the information into one word or a few sentences.

Antique or Collectible Sales. Many people who love antiques and collectibles soon find themselves operating a business from their homes by buying and selling objects they are interested in.

Arts and Crafts Sales. Artists and craftsmen who produce their own artwork and homemade crafts find they can start a home-based business by selling their specialty from their homes, through a catalog, or at special craft sales or fairs.

Association Management Service. Association managers collect dues, keep lists, prepare newsletters, handle mail, keep records, pay bills, raise funds, or perform any other services that an organization hires them to provide.

Auto Detailing. Car detailers provide auto cleaning services that go beyond the neighborhood car wash. Services are limited or expanded according to the desires of the client. Car detailers can work at the client's home or place of employment. Some work for dealers or companies with fleets of cars.

Baking or Catering Service. Home bakers or caterers supply the edibles for a variety of events such as weddings, family reunions, company parties, or any other event where food is needed. (Before starting any type of food business, make sure you comply with public health and safety regulations.)

Bed and Breakfast Inn. If you have an unusual home with extra rooms, enjoy house guests, and have a flair for decorating and cooking, a bed and breakfast inn may be a workable home business.

Bill-Auditing Service. Many companies and individuals need someone to verify their bills by checking orders, making sure goods are delivered according to bills, comparing charges, or checking any number of overcharge possibilities. A bill auditor makes sure all bills are accurate and necessary.

Bookkeeping Service. Bookkeepers handle any part of an organization's or individual's financial records. They often perform payroll and billing services, prepare reports, make deposits, or do any other financial service the client needs.

Business Broker. Business brokers act much like real-estate brokers, but they bring together people who want to sell a business with people who want to buy a business. Most brokers represent the client who is selling a business and obtain a listing agreement with him or her.

Business Network Organizer. One of the best ways to build a business is to develop a network with other business owners. Business network organizers set up and run networking groups to help small-business owners market their businesses to their associates. These networking groups help the members get business for or from each other.

Business Plan Writer. A business plan writer listens to the client's ideas, looks at his or her financial information, then combines all this information into the format of a business plan.

Calligraphy Service. A calligraphy service finds clients who need help writing addresses on envelopes for weddings or filling in names on certificates and diplomas. Calligraphy services can also artistically create favorite quotations suitable for framing or meet other such needs of clients.

Child-Safety Business. A child-safety business would provide a room-by-room check for possible safety problems in private homes. Use research from the Consumer Product Safety Commission for child-safety precautions.

Cleaning Service. House cleaners are more and more in demand as more and more households become two-income families. Commercial or residential cleaning services are always in demand. A cleaning service can specialize in one type of cleaning or generalize, according to the needs of the community.

Collection Agency. Businesses often need help collecting money owed to them. Collection agencies are hired to take care of accounts that are behind in their payments. I know several home-based collection agencies that work exclusively for doctors, but the field is wide open for grocery or retail stores, day-care providers, cable TV operators, and so forth. Collecting money from people is regulated by federal and state laws. Most states require a license.

Computer Consultant. A computer consultant asks his clients what they want to accomplish and then explores the possible ways a computer can help them achieve their desires.

Computer Programmer. A computer programmer prepares the steps or instructions (software or programs) that a computer uses to do something. Applications programmers write programs that solve problems and carry out jobs. Systems programmers write programs that tell the computer how to carry out its own internal operations. Systems analysts help clients find ways to computerize their operations.

Computer Tutor and Trainer. Computer tutors and trainers help people learn how to use computers and computer programs. Training can be with individuals or groups.

Copywriter. Small-business owners seldom have the time to create their own written materials—advertising, brochures, newsletters, and so forth. Copywriters prepare these materials for them.

Corporate Trainer. Companies are finding that to remain competitive, their employees need additional training in many areas. Most trainers specialize. They usually either go to the company and train employees in the workplace, or they hold training meetings at a neutral place where several companies can send employees. Areas of specialty include marketing, sales techniques, computer skills, writing skills, personal time management skills, and a host of others.

Cosmetic Sales. Cosmetic sales are often profitable for home-based people. Most orders are made over the phone.

Diaper Cleaning Service. As more and more parents are becoming "earth friendly," the number of cloth diaper users is climbing, producing a need for cloth diaper services. Most services provide diapers, containers for soiled diapers, and a drop-off and pick-up service at the client's home.

Day-Care Provider. Many working parents prefer the private home day-care option for their children to the large child-care operation that employs many providers at one large facility. A home-based day-care operation is a good choice for someone who wants to stay home with his or her own children and loves working with other children as well.

Desktop Publishing Service. New programs for computers now eliminate typesetting and paste-up. Hundreds of different types of documents are regularly created using desktop publishing.

Desktop Video. With desktop video you can use new technologies to create full-motion videos at your desk. This approach usually combines television and computer technology by mixing computer-generated graphics or text with video images from a camera or videotape. Computers are used for editing. Optical laser software and video equipment like the camcorder make this possible. A desktop-video business might produce television commercials, company videotapes, and visual aids, among many other options.

Disc Jockey Service. Home-based disc jockey services provide professional sound at parties, weddings, and conferences. They provide music for special events in clubs, churches, hotels, public halls, schools, and dances for far less than live musicians. A disc jockey service provides the music, the equipment to play it on, the vehicle to haul the equipment, and an emcee to encourage people to dance.

Editorial Service and Proofreading. Proofreaders check for typographical errors, misspellings, and design specifications after a manuscript has been typeset. Copy editors check grammar, spelling, and syntax; they rewrite text and suggest other changes as needed. Some editors help writers develop or completely rework their ideas.

Entertainment Service. An entertainment service might sell the services of a clown, magician, face painter, singer, dancer, and so forth.

Errand Service. An errand service helps busy people do such errands as grocery shopping, dry cleaning, dropping off and picking up children, running to the post office, picking up prescription medicine, taking people to the airport, and/or other tasks that an individual or company might need help with.

Executive Search. Companies often need someone to match them up with new employees. Executive recruiters are paid by a company to find good people to fill important positions. Most recruiters specialize in one type of industry.

Export Agent. Companies often need someone to be in charge of export sales. Export agents develop relationships with foreign import agents, establishing the business and political contacts they need.

Facialist. Facialists help clients take care of their skin. Facialists often sell skin products as part of their business.

Fitness Trainer. Fitness trainers design workout routines for individuals or small groups. Some trainers take their clients through their workouts and some teach classes in their own homes or in a local gym. Some trainers specialize and work with older people, children, or any special needs group.

Florist. Florists fill their clients' needs to "say it with flowers." Most florists combine fresh-flower arrangements with silk or dried flowers, and many have balloons or other small gifts like candy that can also be delivered for their clients.

Gift Basket Business. For clients who want to say it with something other than flowers or candy, the gift basket business offers a wide variety of home-based delivery services. Gift baskets can be customized to suit the client and may contain food, drink, toys, sporting items, bubble bath, clothing, or any number of choices.

Hairstylist/Manicure Service. People always need a haircut, and the hairstyling home-based business will be around forever. Manicures or other personal appearance services are also often offered.

Hauling Service. If you are the proud owner of a truck or have a close family member or friend who is willing to loan you one, you can help others haul off the junk that won't fit in the city or county garbage bins. Not only are hauling services paid to haul stuff to the dump, but often they can find someone to actually buy the junk!

Herbs, Buying and Selling. This type of home business often starts out as a need to get back to nature. Some health-conscious person starts growing food or herbs and finds that his family and friends are interested in buying the excess.

Home Inspector. Many home buyers want to protect themselves from buying a home with major hidden problems and need someone qualified to check out a place before they get serious. Most inspectors prepare a written report about the condition of the property they inspected. Some home inspectors specialize in certain areas of concern, such as insects, rodents, or structural problems.

Image Consultant. Image consultants help clients select clothing, makeup, and hairstyles. Some consultants help clients with speaking, sitting, and walking skills. Consultants may go directly to their clients' homes and help them organize what they have and decide what is needed by conducting personal interviews and cleaning out closets. Some image consultants work for companies who need large numbers of their employees trained in appearance. Most such consultants help the company develop a visual image and a set of guidelines that employees must follow in dealing with the public.

Indoor Environmental Tester. Indoor environmental testers help individuals or companies decide if their indoor environment is healthy. Individuals with allergies are especially likely to need this service.

Information Retrieval Service. Many individuals and companies need information but lack the necessary skill to obtain it. Like a computer librarian, information brokers locate information quickly. On-line computer databases help get the information, and modems can send it on to the client as quickly as possible.

In-Home Health Care. When patients are not sick enough to be in a hospital but not well enough for outpatient treatment, home-based health care is often the answer. Home-based health care providers take one patient into their homes at a time and help them make the transition between hospital and home. Some mental-health professionals pay families to board a troubled teen for a period of time.

Instructor. People have home-based businesses giving instruction in dance, exercise, sports, music, writing, breeding animals, appraising collections, cooking, canning, child care, arranging flowers, herbs, cake decoration, swimming, and gardening.

Interior Decorator. When home owners redecorate, they often need the help of a professional with fresh new ideas. Interior decorators can charge a flat fee, by the hour, or by a certain percentage of the items they buy. Or they can charge retail price for items they are able to purchase at wholesale and keep the difference as their fee.

Ironing Service. Ironing services come in handy for an increasing number of clients who prefer wash and wear to the high cost of dry cleaning.

Mailing List Service. A mailing list service can create and keep up mailing lists for specific clients, or it can produce its own lists and find clients who need them. Selling monthly updates of these lists is another way to get business.

Mail-Order Business. Mail-order businesses sell products through catalogs or advertisements. Most mail-order businesses that are successful sell items not regularly available through retail stores.

Makeover Service. As more people see makeover results on television and in magazines, makeover specialists find clients who are interested in looking their best for special events. Many makeover services also include a photo-package deal where people can purchase a permanent reminder of what they look like when they have the time and money to hire a professional to help them.

Management Consultant. To be a consultant, you need some sort of expertise that others want and that is not common knowledge or in ready supply. Consultants sell themselves and their special knowledge to businesses or individuals. Fields of consulting range from marketing to educational, from financial to computer, and from health care to public relations.

Medical Billing Service. Many medical professionals need help with their billing, and they can often save money by hiring someone outside the office staff to handle it. A medical biller can also maintain records and process claims for doctors. Much of a doctor's income today comes through billing third-party insurance companies.

Medical Claims Processing Service. Some people do not want to file their own medical claims to insurance companies. Most people know about tax preparation services, but many don't have a clue that someone is willing to handle their medical claims for a fee.

Medical Transcription Service. A transcription service interprets and transcribes dictation by doctors concerning the condition of their patients. Some community colleges offer courses in medical terminology and transcribing, or you can take a home correspondence course.

Newsletter Business. A newsletter is usually a publication that is one to eight pages in length, with a format no larger than 8½ by 11 inches. Newsletters typically are not available on newsstands. Home-based newsletter writers can publish their own special-interest newsletter or produce a newsletter for other people.

Newspaper Delivery Service. Newspaper deliveries are not only for the young. Many homemakers and retired persons enjoy getting paid for their daily exercise.

900–Number Audio-Text Service. To have a successful 900–number business you need a topic that has mass appeal or potential for customers, unique information, and information at a price people are willing to pay. These numbers can provide such information as tax tips, jokes, real estate for sale in an area, and so forth.

Note Reader/Scopist. Court reporters spend the majority of their time in a courtroom or a law office taking notes on a stenograph (machines for writing words phonetically). These notes must be converted into a written transcript. Court reporters often hire note readers or scopists to prepare the transcript for them because they don't have the time.

Paralegal. A paralegal is a legal assistant. They work under the supervision of an attorney and can do anything an attorney does except sign documents, make court appearances in contested proceedings, and give legal advice to clients.

Party Planner. Party-planner services plan events for individuals or for companies. They may plan birthday parties, conventions, fund-raising events, reunions, special banquets, or sales meetings.

Pet-Sitting Service. Some pet sitters go to a client's home to feed the pets, while others live in the home when the residents are away. Pet sitters can also open their homes to a client's pets or operate a pet-sitting facility where clients can bring their pets.

Plant Care Service. Plant sitters operate much like pet sitters in that they go to the client's home to water the plants while the client is away.

Private Investigator. Most private investigators work from their homes; typical clients are lawyers, insurance companies, and business people. The private investigator will do background screens, check references, verify credit, and seek to find missing persons, among other things.

Professional Organizer. Professional organizers organize everything from clutter and closet space to paper, time, and space in general. Some work for individuals in their homes, while others work in professional offices. Organizers usually need to pick a specialty.

Professional-Practice Consultant. Many practicing professionals need a business consultant to handle a variety of concerns, such as billing, collections, personnel, payroll, investments, and even patient scheduling.

Public Relations Specialist. Public relations specialists obtain publicity for their clients in magazines, newspapers, and on radio and television. They produce newsletters, press releases, annual reports, speeches, and brochures that call positive attention to their clients. Many clients can't afford a full-time staff member and contract for this work from freelancers.

Real Estate Appraiser. Real estate appraisers estimate the value of residential and commercial property. Clients need their property appraised before obtaining financing, selling or buying property, after a divorce, and at many other times.

Real Estate Management. Many owners of office buildings, apartments, condos, or homes don't have the time to worry about collecting rent, mowing and watering the lawn, making repairs, and screening new renters. Real estate management services provide the service that a property owner desires.

Repair or Fix-It Service. Home-based repair or fix-it services can include almost anything, from electronic repair, appliance repair, office equipment repair, furniture repair, and so forth. Work can be done on site or a pickup and return service can be offered. For work, you can advertise to potential clients, or make an arrangement with a retailer who needs your services.

Restoration Service. A restoration service caters to clients who want their older homes, businesses, and furniture restored to their original beauty.

Resumé-Writing Service. Many people seeking employment don't have the time or ability to write an effective resumé. A resumé-writing service may create the resumé and/or mail the resumé for the client. Some resumé services also provide employment advice.

Security Consultant. Security consultants provide advice on security policies and make recommendations on security equipment for their clients. They may also be private investigators.

Tax Preparation Service. Most people hate doing their own taxes and many willingly pay someone to do the job for them.

Technical Writer. Technical writers write articles for trade magazines, publicity materials, technical books, and instructional materials. They translate technical information about new products into manuals and booklets that can be easily understood by people who will use them. Many companies hire outside writers to do this work.

Temporary Help Service. Home-based temporary help services usually specialize in supplying a particular type of temporary employee to work for a company. One service may specialize in nurses and another in short-order cooks. Most services obtain their list by running classified ads. Many companies contract with home workers.

Transcript Digesting Service. Before a trial, lawyers take testimony in a deposition recorded by a court reporter. The testimony is transcribed into a document that lawyers can look at before the trial. To save time, the lawyers often hire transcript digesters to identify important points and summarize the transcript.

Travel Agent. Many travel agencies have begun using agents who work from their homes. Special telephone and computer hookups are necessary to tie into the main office, but the company takes care of this arrangement.

Tutor Service. Many students need one-on-one help with subjects they are struggling with in school. Parents or schools hire tutors to work with their children and students. Tutors can help with specific homework assignments or work with a student who has missed instruction due to illness or accident.

Wedding Consultant. A wedding consultant works with the bride and groom and their families to produce the wedding they desire. The consultant oversees florists, photographers, videophotographers, caterers, travel agents, makeup artists, and musicians.

Woodworking. People who enjoy working with wood and producing their own cabinets, shelves, furniture, and toys can run a woodworking business from their home.

Word Processing or Typing Service. Word processing services provide typing for companies that hire outside help. This way the company has to pay only for work produced and can save money. Many home-based word processing services specialize or carve out a niche for themselves. Some provide pickup and delivery service.

Writer. Home-based writers, more commonly known as freelance writers, write for any number of companies or for themselves. Some write books, while others write for magazines and newspapers. Many work as a combination of technical writer and public relations specialist. Writers team up with publishers to get their work to the public.

Those of us who have home-based businesses need to understand the tax laws that apply to us, and we need to keep up with them, because they are always changing. (For information about tax laws for home-based workers, refer to Appendix B.)

There are several ways to start working at home. You can keep a full-time job and develop your home business as a sideline. You can work a part-time job to provide a base income while you're building up a home business. When your home business income equals or passes your outside income, you can drop the outside employment and spend full time on your home business.

If you're expecting a baby, before you leave your job on maternity leave you might ask your boss if you can perform your job at home. Perhaps you can turn your present employer into your first major customer when you strike out on your own.

Finally, keep in mind that a business failure is never the end of world. Even if things don't work out with your home business, your friends and family will still be your friends and family. The world will be the same. You can go on to other things.

WORK OUTSIDE THE HOME—WITHOUT PAY

My father was raised on the Canadian frontier as one of thirteen siblings. Each year before the long Canadian winter, my father's father would take his children up to the mountains to chop enough wood to last through the dark days of snow and cold.

Once, while my dad was watching his father fell a tree, Grandfather turned to my dad and said, "Heber, chop your own wood and it will warm you twice."

My dad began to understand his father only when he noticed that he was growing warmer and warmer the harder he worked at chopping the logs. Later that winter, when my dad was relaxing in front of the wood stove in the kitchen reading a favorite book, he realized that the wood he chopped was his source of warmth. When he saw the comfort the logs gave to the other members of his family and friends, his understanding was finally complete.

Unpaid work outside our homes, or volunteer work, warms us twice. Volunteers have the vision to see others as part of their larger family; they have the compassion to see the needs of those around them in their neighborhoods, cities, and nations. Hospitals, schools, and community programs are crying for people who have time to give.

After my grandmother raised a large family, she volunteered her time at the local hospital rocking newborn babies in the nursery. When my neighbor retired, he volunteered as a grandpa helper at the local elementary school.

One well-to-do man told me that the most liberating thing he had ever done was to go through his house and give away everything he did not need. Not only did his house look better, but he told me he suddenly lost the desire to be a workaholic when he realized how little he truly needed to survive. His wife was upset at first, but she soon caught the vision. Before long she lost her desire to spend most of her time shopping and redecorating their lavish home.

This couple began volunteering their time in the community and helping extended family members. They donated money to worthy causes anonymously. When they went out to dinner, they selected a family in the restaurant and paid for their meal. When they went to a movie, they picked out several couples behind them in line and paid for their tickets.

Volunteerism can free us from the trap of desiring financial payment for all the work we do.

WORK OUTSIDE THE HOME—FOR PAY

"What are you going be when you grow up?" I heard my young son ask his brother the other day. "You still want to be a geologist?"

"Yeah," Joseph answered. Joseph has been smashing rocks for years now.

There was a long pause. "I still don't know what I want to do yet," Jacob answered. "But I'm sure I want to, well, I want to do something interesting."

We all ought to do something interesting when we grow up. Work is not just what we do for pay but something we do with life. All of us have to answer the question, "What will my work be?"

Yet work, any work, can be something interesting if our minds make it so. All work is meaningful when done for the right reason. All honest work is honorable.

It doesn't matter what type of paid work we do outside our

homes if we do it honestly and with genuine affection for those we serve. I know people who have been able to wash away their tears in sweat. Work is a blessing, a way to provide for our own and our family's physical, emotional, and spiritual needs.

The most important decisions concerning paid employment outside the home have little to do with *what* we choose for a career or *how much* we are paid. Most of us live well from a material perspective. But do we live nobly? Life is more than a balance sheet of financial gain and loss. Our decisions concerning paid employment should transcend unbridled ambition, careerism, and materialism.

We escape the false god of career when, *first*, we decide to work. No one owes us a living. Healthy adults are responsible to provide food, shelter, and clothing for themselves and the next generation. All parents should obtain the skills or education to financially provide for their families. A good education and up-to-date training are vital to both parents, even if only one is working for pay at the present time.

But a career is not a life. A career is something we do to sustain life. Problems occur in paid employment when we fail to understand the equally important work of our hearts. We forget our eternal purpose in life when we throw ourselves off balance by spending too much time earning a living and not enough time living.

Like the hub of a wheel, each of us has centrifugal forces that can spin us out of control. Yet we can remain still—at peace with ourselves and God—if we give balanced attention to all important areas of our lives, physically, intellectually, socially, and spiritually. My spirit needs me to simplify my physical life, shed unnecessary distractions, and decide what is essential and what I can do without.

Second, we can't let our role as providers for our children snuff out our other important roles as nurturers and teachers. Our children need nourishment for their bodies, but they also need nourishment for their souls. Work is important to our happiness, but it can also become our escape from our inner selves, family, and neighbors. Work is an essential part of balancing our lives, but we err when we place it at our center.

If we sacrifice time with our families to the god of ambition and career, we have lost sight of our true vocation. Children give parents entrance to their hearts, and we need to remember that when we are welcome there, we are on holy ground.

Third, we must never define our worth by what we do for a living, but instead by the meaning we bring to the work. When we work with our hands and our hearts, we begin to find one of the greatest joys in life. Life is not a large black hole of impossible human happiness, but a great vast open field of possibilities for us to work toward the happiness of our human family. The truest reward from work is not what we get, but what we become. We do our best not always because the work is worth it, but because we are. If we work only for the wage, we have chosen work that pays us little.

A broader vision of work comes when we discover joy today as we glimpse a future we desire. The drudgery comes when we find no joy in our efforts now and cannot glimpse a desirable future. By doing our common work uncommonly and with love, we take the drudgery out of it.

Once a woman walked past a neighborhood construction site, waved, and yelled, "Whatcha all doing?"

"I'm making ten bucks an hour," one worker shouted.

"I'm wrecking my back," a second added.

"I'm building a beautiful new home," the third man in bib overalls replied. (His two co-workers jabbed him in the ribs.)

The important consideration is not so much what we do as how we *think* about what we do. Work is a blessing to us and those we serve if we make it so. We underestimate the power of our influence if we choose to focus on the work of our hands to the neglect of the work of our hearts.

The people of Nazareth once said, "Is not this the carpenter?" (Mark 6:3.)

They saw the work of Christ's hands but they failed to see his most important work.

"This is my work and my glory—to bring to pass the immortality and eternal life of man." (Moses 1:39.)

Fourth, we should remember the Sabbath, for it is a celebration of life, a weekly reminder that the world does not own us, that men and women are made for rest, prayer, study, and holiness just as we are made for production and creating. The order of the first creation modeled for us the necessity of work first . . . then rest. The rest of one day in seven is vital for the *re-creation* of our souls.

When I'm out on a bicycle ride with my husband, I often find myself wishing for a trek that is downhill both going and coming back. But I have learned that I must go up a hill before I descend. I must work before I can appreciate the sweetness of rest.

At some point in our lives, we will all meet with disillusionment in our chosen professions. We will yearn for something more than wanting, working, and possessing. We can live lives filled with hope, gratitude, thanksgiving, and celebration if we remember that work has nothing to do with our job titles or our take-home pay and everything to do with faith, vision, and love.

IT'S TRUE—WORK REALLY IS A BLESSING

When I was young I remember saying, every time my mother gave me a job to do, "If work is a blessing, I must be the most blessed kid in the whole world."

As a middle child in a family of nine, my introduction to the world of work began at a young age. I was about five years old when my mother assigned me to scrub the sink in the bathroom. Not so willingly, I marched to the bathroom, selected a sponge under the sink cabinet, and went to work. There was a spot in the bottom of the sink I couldn't seem to get rid of no matter how hard I scrubbed.

I walked back into the kitchen, located my mother, and whined, "There's a spot in the sink and I can't get it out."

"Well, use a little more elbow grease," my mother replied matter-of-factly as she finished the dishes.

I dragged my face back into the bathroom, all the while wondering where I could find the elbow grease my mother had advised me to use. I searched under the sink and found something I thought might fit the bill. I walked back to the kitchen carrying a canister of some unknown substance and approached my mother again.

"Is this elbow grease?" I asked.

My mother looked down at me and laughed. I couldn't figure out what was so funny. People were always laughing at me when I wasn't trying to be funny and frowning at me when I was trying to be funny. Obviously, I surmised, whatever I had selected wasn't right, so I dragged my feet back to the bathroom and searched one more time. Nothing else under the sink looked anything like elbow grease.

Then the light came on in my head. If I couldn't find it under the sink, maybe elbow grease was some special substance manufactured by real elbows. I looked down at my own elbow and searched for something resembling cleaning solvent. Then I lowered my elbow into the sink and began rubbing it vigorously on the spot. Still nothing. I was completely disappointed. If I'd been a little older, I might have uttered something like the famous words spoken by Shakespeare's Lady Macbeth, but at five years of age, I just cried.

Later, my mother finally explained the definition of elbow grease. I learned that elbow grease is not something you find under the sink or a cleaning solvent produced by your elbow. Elbow grease means you work a little harder and not stop until you've got the job done. I've been required to work a few times since that day in the bathroom, and I've discovered that good old-fashioned labor still works wonders.

If we want our children to be happy, we need to remember their need to work and be useful. When children learn to work while they're growing up, they feel needed. If parents want their children to enjoy doing the everyday chores of life, they will work with their children, encourage them, and praise their efforts.

All our children have jobs inside and outside our home. They mow lawns, clean houses and offices, babysit, deliver newspapers, work at local businesses, make beds, fix meals, clean clothes, weed gardens, and help local farmers.

One day after my daughter came home from a long day at the video-pizza store where she works, she told me that her work had given her a new appreciation for all the working people in the world. She also said it had given her a new confidence that she could work hard to earn the things she really wanted in life, like a good education.

Work is what we spend our energy on to accomplish something. The opposite of work isn't play. Play is as necessary for a full, rich life as work. The opposite of work is idleness, or the conscious decision *not* to accomplish anything.

Some of our greatest joys will come from the work we choose as worthy expressions of our time and talents both inside and outside the home. Satisfaction comes in the process of choosing work that is challenging and serves family and neighbors at the same time.

The happiest people understand that work is a blessing and a personal expression of gratitude for the gift of life.

CHAPTER 5

We Are Stewards, Not Owners

And why take ye thought for raiment?
Consider the lilies of the field, how they
grow; they toil not, neither do they spin;
And yet I say unto you, That even
Solomon in all his glory was not arrayed
like one of these.

—MATTHEW 6:28–29

FLIGHT

Once there was a woman who thought she loved birds. When the woman was feeling lonely, she would go for a walk in the mountains close to her home. When she got tired, she would sit under a shady tree and hold very still. If she held very still for a long time, she could hear the wind washing through the leaves of the tree overhead. If she held very still for an even longer time, a bird would come to the tree and sing.

Soon the woman bought some binoculars and a book about birds. She learned the names and habits of all the birds in her mountains and spent long hours listening to them sing. When the sun went down and the mountains became cold and dark, the woman would go home and sit by the fire and draw pictures of birds.

One day the woman said, "If I could only have my own wild bird, then I could draw even better pictures and I would not be alone or sad anymore."

So the woman obtained a net and took it with her the next time she went to the mountains. She went on a hike until she was very tired; then she stopped to rest under a large shady tree. First she heard the wind washing through the leaves, and then she heard a bird singing. The woman took the net and laced it over the tree very quietly. Then she shook the tree and a startled bird flew into the net.

"Now I have a bird of my own to take home and take care of, and I'll never be alone or sad again," the woman said.

So the woman took the bird home and gently raised the net off its wings. The bird was tired and sick from struggling to escape, so the woman had an easy time placing the bird in the beautiful golden cage she had prepared.

"You will be happy here," the woman said. "I will tend you and feed you and draw beautiful pictures of you. Someday your picture will appear in full-color illustrated books about birds."

The bird wasn't listening. The bird was thinking about his home in the mountains and the wind and the trees. The woman put a blanket over the cage and went to bed. The next morning she went into her studio and began to draw a picture of the bird.

"Don't lie there so still," the woman said to the bird. "Stand up and spread your wings so I can draw your brilliant colors and catch the grace of your movement."

The bird was not listening. He would not move or stretch his wings because he was thinking about home. The woman was concerned, so she bought ultra-premium birdseed in a velvet-lined dish, but the bird would not eat. Once the bird scratched the woman, and she got angry and shook the cage.

"You don't appreciate everything I've done for you," the woman said. "You are a selfish, tiresome creature and I hate you."

The woman was crabby when she went to bed that night. The next morning the woman went into her studio and found the bird very still at the bottom of the cage.

"If you don't eat, you will die," the woman said. "You are my bird now and you will do what I say. Sing, and be happy, you stupid bird."

The bird did not sing and the woman didn't feel much like drawing. Many days passed, and the bird grew weaker and weaker.

The woman was worried.

"I will take you back to the mountains," the woman finally said.

The woman put the bird in her car and drove to her

favorite spot in the mountains. She hiked with the cage on her back until she become very tired. Then she rested under a large, shady tree.

The woman opened the door to the cage and the bird flew away. She left the cage under the tree and hiked back down to her car. The woman felt tired and sad when she arrived home.

Several days later, before the woman got out of bed in the morning, she suddenly heard a strange tapping sound outside her window. When she looked up, she saw the bird stretching his wings on her windowsill just as the morning sunlight caught the brilliant colors of his feathers.

The woman sat up in bed and smiled. Then she reached under her bed and took out her sketchbook and quickly drew a magnificent picture of the bird before it flew away.

"You are not mine," the woman said as she watched the bird disappear into the sky. "Thank you for coming to me. You are beautiful. You are free."

In the afternoons, the woman went hiking in the mountains with her sketchbook. In time she grew fond of many wild birds, but she did not try to catch them. She drew many wonderful pictures of birds as they would land on her shoulder or eat from her hands. But she did not try to keep them.

The people in town called her the bird woman because birds were always filling the air around her house, following her wherever she walked, and singing in her trees.

Once there was a woman who thought she loved birds. And she did. 🕊

THE BURDEN OF OWNERSHIP

One warm summer evening, soon after we had carpeted the basement of our new home, our neighbor fell asleep and let his irrigation water run too long in the hay field next to our house. By morning, smelly brown water was rapidly filling our basement.

While I was downstairs frantically trying to keep water out of my house with a wet/dry vacuum and a mountain of towels, I found myself fuming at the irresponsibility of my neighbor. And I felt totally justified in my anger.

"We've worked hard all our lives for a nice house and a few acres," I thought to myself. "Then somebody or something comes along and ruins everything."

My husband and I had saved for years to afford this place. Our dream had always been to find a home large enough for our family of ten, with a few acres away from the crowded city and noise. We wanted the freedom to enjoy nature and surround ourselves with a garden and fruit trees.

I remembered the day we first moved in. I stood alone on the back acre next to the wild plum trees thinking, "All this is mine."

I mentally walked around the boundaries of our land, making note of each tree or rock, taking mental possession.

I found a piece of garbage and threw it over the fence, thinking, "Well, at least it's not in my field now."

Then I looked at the field next to me and began wishing I had the money to buy my neighbor's land. What I didn't realize at that moment was that I had just planted all the seeds of unhappiness.

After that long, traumatic day cleaning up after the flood, I once again walked to our back acre next to the wild plum trees and surveyed my property. I knew I had come here to be free and already my possessions were possessing me. I didn't own this house and this land; this house and land owned me.

As I stood alone in the field that day, tired and aching after my frantic efforts to rescue all my things from our flooded basement, something inside me began to question my way of seeing.

Deep inside, I knew I could lose every possession I owned and still be perfectly happy if I made up my mind to be. Everything I valued most still surrounded me. I hadn't lost anything of real value. My life, family, work, and friends all seemed like old companions I suddenly rediscovered I loved, not because I owned them, but because they were freely given gifts to cherish.

I sat down in the field and cupped my hands around the lush barley and clover leaves next to me, contemplating that everything within and without my palms was indeed a quiet miracle. That day, I began to understand that I could enjoy my neighbor's field as well as my own. I knew I couldn't afford to invest the rest of my life in more things—to sell my life for so little.

I longed to burst out of myself, to leave my measuring and metering of love with the expectation of equal return. I longed to tear down the fences between me and my neighbor. In my mind, I imagined that all the fields surrounding my home were invisibly connected with a single thread, spiraling out from me for millions of miles. I realized, for the first time, that the fence lines were only a temporary illusion. I felt like I'd been a blind man in a world of wonder.

I understood that what matters most can never be taken away. If someone can ruin or steal it, then it was never really ours to start with. Our homes, lands, possessions, and children pass through our hands and hearts, but they are not ours. We may have stewardship over them for a few short years but we do not own them.

I'd spent most of my life suffocating in ownership and wasting my energies on acquiring more things. But even after I'd acquired a possession, it was difficult to enjoy it because ownership is such hard work. I had to worry about my things, keep my things clean, pay taxes on my things, repair my things, store my things, worry about losing my things, and try to figure out how to make my things bigger and better.

As a young woman, I spent a summer in Israel digging up Beersheba as an archaeological volunteer. Beersheba was a walled community in ancient times, but now it is an archaeological excavation site surrounded by nomadic Arabic tribes. While we volunteers studied the rise and fall of many powerful, wealthy ancient

civilizations in our afternoon university classes at the site, I realized
the Bedouins were the only ancient civilization that still existed.

All a Bedouin possesses must be carried from place to place as
he follows the herds. Ownership is a literal burden. Those who truly
understand the burden of ownership make careful choices.
"Possession restraint" has given the Bedouin the ability to survive
through many generations while all other wealthy cultures and civilizations have fallen.

SEEING THE BEAUTY AND BLESSINGS

I believe we uncover the place of rest deep inside us when we
allow a space in our hearts for gratitude, when we open ourselves
to the realization of life's abundance. We are never truly prosperous until we realize that our lives are full of riches that money can't
buy. Life is a gift, a precious gift. Knowing the trip is always too short
lends an urgency to our awareness. There is a child in our hearts
we need to discover before it's time to leave.

As I walked back to my house, that evening after our basement
flood, I felt like a child once again—eager to learn, see, touch, and
feel. I no longer desired new possessions but new eyes. The earth's
beauty is an open treasure for those who see.

There's a certain early morning light that brushes the tops of
cornstalks and barley fields east of my home. Every spring and summer, as I look out over the shimmering fields, I wonder if the farmers who work this ground have any idea how much pleasure they
give me. Strangers unknowingly fill my life with such gladness.

When I slow my living enough to see the good things, I realize
there are nothing but miracles: the man who sleeps beside me,
chocolate milkshakes, schoolchildren with shining eyes, old books,
trees bowed down with ripe peaches, new socks, the stranger at the
grocery store who smiles and says howdy, elbows, microwave ovens,
peace roses blooming in the front yard, birds, a newborn's first cry,
poetry, the man in a cowboy hat who waves from his truck, music,
computers that check spelling, indoor plumbing, and rainbows.

On my better days, when I am able to see what is real, I understand that I live in an age of wonders—from the space shuttle flights to my miraculous ability to breathe, see, walk, feel, hear, and touch. That we exist at all speaks of something far greater than any of us understands. If we're not paying attention, we'll miss the joy.

I once knew a woman named Blanche who was confined to bed because of a stroke. While I was in bed because of premature labor a few years ago, we became telephone buddies. Before bed confinement, Blanche had been confined to a wheelchair for thirty years because of a doctor's drunken mistake on the surgery table. After she returned home from the surgery, her husband left because he was unable to deal with the added responsibilities. Blanche raised four children alone in her wheelchair. She had every reason to focus on what she had lost. Instead, she chose to focus on what she had.

Blanche had one window in her bedroom from which she could see a single tree. During our telephone conversations, Blanche would describe in intimate detail the intricate changes the seasons would bring to her tree.

"It's such a miracle to be able to see," Blanche said. "I have so much to live for."

Blanche used the same detailed descriptions when she spoke of her grandchildren. She saw beauty and blessings everywhere she looked because she chose to see with new eyes, even though her entire landscape was only a tiny bedroom.

If I had been Blanche, I would have been a tad upset that I couldn't walk or get out of bed. But Blanche knew that the only true power we possess is the ability to see life as it really is. Life as it really is, is downright amazing.

Blanche often called me to wish me a happy Thursday at 2:15 P.M. or a happy Monday at 10:45 A.M. She didn't wait for holidays or birthdays to celebrate or share her love of life. She understood that we have to be in charge of our own joy and create our own celebrations of life.

Blanche is gone now. On my lonely days, I like to think about her and try to see the world as she would have seen it. Even though she had only a tiny bedroom window to open her eyes, Blanche knew about miracles. If she were here, she'd wish us all a happy today. But right now—well, I figure Blanche is square dancing in heaven.

Sometimes we allow ownership to trap us in adulthood. We have to hold fast to the child within as the years dissolve before our eyes; we have to reawaken the faith we had long ago before we lost our ability to see what mattered most—before we became disillusioned by facts and figures, profit and loss.

My husband and I were doing some remodeling at our home a while back. We ripped out windows, boards, and carpet, making a terrible mess. At one point, all that remained of the one-time playroom over our garage was bones. The trusses, studs, and floor resembled the inside of a whale's belly. Because we live at the mouth of Spanish Fork Canyon, we often get a hefty canyon breeze in the morning. House skeletons let the wind blow through—and the rain and the dirt and the bugs and a few other things. But, strange as it may sound, I found myself enjoying the openness.

Before long, we had the room all sealed up with plywood, insulated windows, doors, and walls. We soon had our security from the wind, rain, and dirt, but I found myself left with the strangest feeling of longing. Insulated rooms, or people, don't let hummingbirds inside.

One day before we completed the walls, I was down on my hands and knees scrapping off the remains of the old carpet when a hummingbird flew into the exposed room and hovered next to me. I held my breath and remained perfectly still so I wouldn't frighten the tiny bird away. Hummingbirds are my favorite.

That little bird reminded me that once, long before, when I was a small child, I saw something beautiful darting up and down, back and forth near the lilac bush in our backyard. That night in our bunk beds, I told my older sister in a hushed voice that I'd seen a real live fairy. She laughed and told me I needed glasses.

The wonder and fascination didn't end there. When I later discovered fairies were really hummingbirds, I wrote a detailed report in third grade that included several elaborate drawings of the hummingbird's hover patterns and a cross-section view of the bird's forked tongue. For the cover of my report, I spent hours drawing a ruby-throated hummingbird perched in mid-air, with its long, slender bill inside a honeysuckle flower.

As I watched that delicate bird in our bare-bones room, I noticed the wings were beating so fast they became a blur and made a humming sound. I remembered that hummingbird wings can move up to seventy times a second; I remembered that sometimes hummingbirds steal insects from spider's webs and use the threads from the web to build a soft nest for eggs no larger than navy beans. I still believe hummingbirds are the closest living relative to fairies.

If my husband and I had finished bracing the walls before that day, my reminder of the magic of childhood would have remained outside. Hummingbirds remind me to be full of wonder and awe. They remind me to look freshly at common things. They remind me how quickly we lose our desire to fly.

I was born with a pure sense of wonder, a belief that everything was possible. I once had a pure instinct for what is beautiful and awe inspiring. The emptiness of adulthood came as I forgot the magic of flight and grounded myself with the things of this earth. Maybe I'll never be able to truly believe in fairies again, but I can remember how it felt when I did. I can begin again to relish the richness and diversity of my everyday life by becoming more like my children—more aware, observant, and free.

Our whale's belly room let the sun shine in, and the wind and the rain. Now, even after the walls have gone up and the insulation has been carefully stapled in place, I can remember the hummingbird that came inside that day. After we've grown up and our walls have gone up and our insulation against pain has been carefully stapled in place, we can open the windows and let the wonder of life burst back into ourselves. We can invite the hummingbirds and magic back inside.

Stewardship includes a sacred accountability to acknowledge our blessings. Sometimes our greatest blessings are hidden behind our greatest challenges. I often have to do my writing after midnight because, frankly, it's the only time when my house is quiet and nobody needs anything from me—like a meal, acceptance, diaper change, conversation, clean clothes, affection, the car, patience, or permission to punch their brother. Though my large, demanding family makes it difficult to find time to write, my large, demanding family also provides me with the growth that gives me something to say.

I live in the country. It's dark up here on the bench at night, but it is that very darkness that allows me to see the stars with a clarity and brightness the city folks miss. The sleepless lights of modern civilization are out of my line of view and keep my nights black, moonlit, and full of wonder. I, too, often fail to see heaven's light at midday. Only in darkness do my brightest stars shine forth.

When I'm up late at night because of illness, work, or babies, I've often longed to rise up like one of Charles Dickens' ghosts and pass among the houses down in the valley. Out there in the darkness, I know I'd find other exhausted mothers and fathers trying to soothe newborn babies to sleep. I know I'd find grandparents tossing restlessly between the sheets of age and that passing we call death. I know I'd find weary-eyed fathers waiting for lost sons and weary-eyed sons waiting for lost fathers. We live lives of remarkable similarity—each full of joy and pain, loss and gain. Our most sacred stewardships are surprisingly similar. We are brothers and sisters all searching for a light in the darkness.

Every night before I go to bed, I steal silently through the dark house and check on each of my children. There is nothing more beautiful than a sleeping child. Then I climb the stairs to the living room, part the curtains next to the sofa, and look up. In that quiet, unclaimed period outside of time, I let go of today before I have to embrace tomorrow. I remind myself that light will follow darkness, no matter how long the night.

WHAT MATTERS MOST CAN NEVER BE OWNED

Our attitude toward ownership and our understanding of stewardship while we're raising our families will profoundly affect the quality of our lives. Income is not important. Possessions are not important. There are happy families who live in grass huts. There are unhappy families who live in mansions. There are also unhappy families who live in grass huts and happy families who live in mansions.

It takes wisdom and planning to make wise choices. If we keep our focus on possessions and wealth, we will ultimately meet with hopelessness and despair. If we have grateful hearts and seek the kingdom of God, we are promised all this and heaven too.

Families are in a constant state of change. Parents never get the chance to slow any growing season. Children grow up. Parents grow old. One generation dissolves into the next. Even in all this continual transformation, families give the ultimate purpose and meaning to our lives. Our families (and our greater family includes all of us) are the ultimate light in the darkness.

Ashley, my two-year-old, and Amy, my four-year-old, were having a heated argument the other day while they discussed the ownership of a certain doll.

"Mine!" both girls screamed, each pulling on the doll until it lost an arm and a leg. They dropped the doll, moved on to greener pastures, and fought over a book. Before the book lost an expensive binding, I tried to explain that the book belonged to all of us. It didn't help much.

"Mine!" both girls insisted.

We don't change much even after we grow up.

"Mine!" husbands and wives insist.

"Mine!" nations insist.

"Mine!" "Mine!" "Mine!"

My four-year-old and I struggled with the question of ownership again later that week.

"Look at those flowers," Amy said, pointing to the neighbor's daisies early one morning. "Can I pick some?"

"I'm sorry, Amy," I answered. "But those flowers don't belong to us. They belong to the neighbors."

I was busy weeding the shrubs circling our front yard. Amy lowered her eyebrows and looked puzzled. I could tell she didn't understand.

"Our neighbors planted those flowers and they take care of them, so we can't pick them because they aren't ours," I added, trying to clarify the issue. "But we can enjoy the flowers. We don't have to own something to enjoy it."

Amy shook her head, walked over to the cement steps in front of our house, and sat down. She wrapped her arms around her knees and surveyed the front yard with new eyes.

"Who owns that pine tree?" Amy asked.

"We do," I answered, standing up. "Well, at least we're supposed to own the pine tree because it's on our property, but someone else planted it, and everybody can drive by and enjoy it."

I walked over and sat down next to Amy.

"Who owns that mother bird and her baby birds in the nest in the pine tree?" Amy asked again.

"Well, as far as I know, no one owns the birds," I answered. "The birds are wild and free to fly away whenever they want to."

Amy lowered her eyebrows, turning the gears in her head again.

"But they're in *our* tree," she responded.

"That's true, Amy, but some things just can't be owned," I said.

Amy looked up past the tree and studied the sky. She squinted, then followed a low-hanging storm cloud drifting along the foothills on the horizon.

"Who owns the sky?" Amy asked.

"Well, no one owns the sky," I answered. "The sky is just there for everybody. It's too big and important for anyone to own."

Amy seemed pleased. She smiled, then glanced down at her sandals.

"Who owns these sandals?" Amy asked, wiggling her toes.

"You do," I answered. "I bought those sandals for you, so you own the sandals. But many, many people worked to make those sandals for you. So, in a way, those sandals connect you to all of the people who helped make them, and you're just a part owner."

The wind caught Amy's hair and whipped it into her eyes. She brushed her golden hair from her face.

"Who owns the wind?" Amy asked.

"No one owns the wind," I answered. "No one will ever be able to catch all the wind and keep it for themselves. The wind is free for everyone. It is too big and powerful for someone to own. Even though we can't see the wind, we know it's real when we see the leaves on the tree move and feel it dance in our hair."

Amy thought for a long while, then turned her face to mine.

"Who owns me?" Amy asked.

I wasn't sure how to answer that one. I had to think for a minute.

"No one owns you, Amy," I finally answered. "You are free like the birds and the sky and the wind. You need a home like those baby birds need that nest. Your mom and dad will take care of you and teach you until you're ready to fly."

"Did you pay for me?" Amy asked again.

"The doctor and hospital wanted money," I answered. "Dad and Mom have to pay money for the house you live in, the clothes you wear, and the food you eat. But you, Amy, you came free."

Amy smiled. The wind made goose bumps rise on our arms.

"I love you like the wind, Amy," I said, drawing her close. "You can't buy love; it has to be free. Love is too big and powerful for anyone to own. You can't see it, but you know it's there because you can feel it."

Amy nestled her head in the bend of my arm. Wind rustled the towering poplar trees behind us. Seagulls filled the air in synchronized flight above the freshly irrigated field before us.

We are stewards, not owners. The earth and its fullness is a gift to everyone. Though we stake our boundaries with fences, though we seek to build up our wealth in houses, cars, and bank accounts, we are only fooling ourselves.

A meaningful life is always potluck. If we bring love and gratitude to the table, there will always be a plentiful feast. He that has "a merry heart hath a continual feast." (Proverbs 15:15.)

Only what we bring to the table and freely share will at last nourish us. Happiness comes from a capacity to feel deeply and enjoy simple things. True joy is not in things but in us. Money has never been required to buy even one necessary nourishment for our soul.

If we exercise childlike faith and believe that all things will work together for our good, they will. If we remember that the most important things in life are not things, but people—and if we avoid debt, give to ourselves and others, see work as a blessing, and understand the nature of stewardship—we can live full, meaningful lives. The best things in life can't be bought, sold, or saved.

Welcome to life's table. There is enough for all of us.

Financial Terms

As you develop your family's financial plans, here are some terms you should be familiar with:

SAVINGS AND INVESTMENTS

CD. The certificate of deposit, CD, is a savings instrument issued by a financial institution that pays you interest at a guaranteed rate for a specified term. When the CD reaches maturity, you will receive your principal and all interest earned.

Money Market Account. A money market account is tied to short-term securities. The interest rate on the money market account responds quickly to changes in financial and economic conditions.

Real Estate. A home mortgage is a loan you secure from a bank or individual to buy a home. You agree to make monthly payments. In the event you do not make your monthly payments, the bank or individual has the legal right to take possession of the home.

Terms to be familiar with include:

Origination fee—A one-time charge that the lender will add as a cost of the mortgage.

Simple interest rate—This is the quoted rate of the loan. If a mortgage is negotiated for 25 years at 11 percent with a 3 point origination fee, the simple interest is still 11 percent.

Effective interest rate—This is different from the simple rate in that it is the *actual* cost of borrowing, including origination fees.

PITI—This stands for the total monthly payment of principal, interest, taxes, and insurance.

Capital gains—The profits from the sale of real estate.

Depreciation/Appreciation—The decline or increase in the value of a piece of property over time.

There are substantial tax benefits associated with mortgage interest and property tax payments. There are also savings benefits with home ownership, because the equity you build up as you pay for your home will probably represent a sizable nest egg by the time you sell. With the traditionally upward trend in real estate prices, you'll probably find the value of your home will increase substantially over the years.

Making money in real estate usually requires that you use as little of your own money as possible. However, leveraged real estate investments are risky because real estate is not liquid, making it difficult to get out of a poor investment or to liquidate when the business cycle is low.

Rental property expenses such as advertising, heating, fuel, water, painting, repairs, and property taxes are business expenses. You subtract them from the gross rents and pay no taxes on them. You can also subtract the depreciation allowance allowable by law. You can take the maximum allowable depreciation as quickly as you can and then sell the property. Mortgage interest is another tax-deductible business expense on rental properties.

Land does not wear out, so you can't depreciate it. You may *invest* in real estate, but you *speculate* in land. If there is no current income from the land, it just sits there and accumulates property taxes.

A real estate investment trust, or REIT, makes use of pooled funds to invest in real estate properties much as mutual funds pool investors' money to buy stock market securities. One type of REIT invests in the equity of real estate properties; another, which invests in mortgages, is a fixed-income type of security.

Stocks and Bonds. Stock represents a unit of ownership in a corporation. When you buy stock, you are becoming a part owner of a business.

A bond is a form of debt issued by a government or a corporation. In exchange for a sum of money lent by the buyer of the bond, the issuer of the bond promises to pay a specific amount of interest at stated intervals for a specific period of time. At the end of the repayment period, the issuer repays the amount of money borrowed.

RETIREMENT PLANS

401(k). The 401(k) is known as the deferred salary reduction plan; it allows an employee to set aside part of his or her salary into a tax-sheltered account that grows tax free until withdrawal. Unlike the IRA, 401(k) must be set up by the employer, who will often make matching contributions on behalf of their employees.

While the IRA's annual contribution limit is $2,000 per year, you and your employer can make a combined investment contribution to your 401(k) plan of up to $9,500 per year or 25 percent of your salary (whichever is less).

With an IRA, you indicate the size of your contribution as a deductible on your federal income forms. With 401(k), this is not necessary. Your contribution is deducted from the income reported on your W-2 form. However, the full salary is still subject to Social Security tax.

Annuity. The annuity may be considered the opposite of a traditional life insurance policy. When you buy insurance, you agree to pay annual premiums to an insurance company. In return, the company will pay the face value of the policy in a lump sum to your beneficiaries when you die. By contrast, when you buy an annuity, you pay the company a lump sum of money and, in return, you receive income for as long as the contract specifies.

IRA. An individual retirement account, IRA, is a method of investing that was originally designed to help individuals not covered by company pension plans. In 1982, the law changed to make IRAs available to anyone with earned income. The law changed again in 1987 to limit the amount deductible from your income. The annual contribution limit to an IRA is $2,000.

Keogh. The Keogh is a saving or investment plan for self-employed persons; its purpose and benefits resemble those of the IRA, except the Keogh plan allows a larger amount of money to be sheltered from income taxes each year. The Keogh plan is a form of pension plan designed for the self-employed individual, whether he works full or part time. Even though you work for another employer full time, if you have any income from self-employment you can contribute part of it to your Keogh plan.

A Keogh plan account is similar to an IRA. Your annual contribution reduces your taxable income and the sums grow tax free until you withdraw the investment. Early withdrawals, before age 59 1/2, carry a 10 percent penalty. The IRA maximum equals $2,000 per year. The annual Keogh maximum equals $30,000 or 25 percent of earned income. In a "money purchase" plan, a fixed percentage of your income is taken out each year. In a "profit-sharing" plan, you are allowed to make varying contributions each year—the tax-deductible limit is 13.043 percent of your self-employment earnings, up to a maximum of $30,000.

SEP. The simplified employee pension, SEP, is a pension-plan approach that can help business owners, including those who are self-employed, to achieve financial security for retirement. Authorized by Congress in 1978, SEP gives small business (even self-employed workers without employees) a program of current tax deduction and future pension benefits.

With SEP, the business sets up an IRA for each employee and makes an annual contribution—up to $30,000 or 15 percent (13.043 percent for self-employed) of earnings.

INSURANCE AND WILLS

Life Insurance. The basic purpose of life insurance is to offer financial protection to your loved ones in the event of your death.

Term life offers the greatest initial amount of financial protection at the lowest cost in premiums. As you grow older, however, the cost of the protection increases.

Whole life insurance is a straight policy that offers a specified death benefit (the face value of the policy) in exchange for unchanging premium payments.

Wills. A will is a set of instructions about what should be done with your property after you die. If you fail to prepare a properly executed will, your property may not be distributed as you hoped it would be, your heirs may suffer a greater tax burden and higher administrative costs, and your family and friends may be subject to needless worry and contention.

Tax Rules for Home-Based Workers

If you're going to work at home for pay, there are some things you need to know about taxes. Please understand that I offer these not as tax advice, but only as things you need to consider.

DEDUCTIONS FOR THE HOME-BASED WORKER

You can deduct the cost of operating and maintaining the part of your home that you use for business. The IRS has two basic criteria your home office must meet in order to qualify as a tax write-off. The first is that the portion of your home that you wish to claim as a business expense must be used *exclusively* and *regularly* for business. There are two exceptions to the exclusive-use rule. You may take a deduction for space used to store inventory and for space used as a day-care facility.

The second criterion is that the portion of the home you use exclusively and regularly for business must be either your principal place of business or a place where you meet with customers or clients in the normal course of business. A "principal place of business" means that, if you have more than one place where you conduct business, your home must be the primary place if you wish to be able to claim it as a deduction.

Direct expenses for the business portion of your home are fully deductible. But the IRS makes a distinction between capital improvements (like adding a room that you use for business, installing customized cabinets in your home office, or designing space for your computer) and repairs that you'd make in the normal course of maintenance (like fixing a broken window or repainting your office).

Repairs are deductible capital improvements which are depreciated. That means the deduction must be spread over a period of several years. Indirect expenses related to the entire home—such as mortgage payments, insurance, utility bills, exterior painting, and roof repair are deductible in part. To calculate the part of these expenses you can deduct, divide the square footage of your office space by the total square footage of the home. You can also calculate the deductible portion of your home by dividing the number of rooms used for business by the total number of rooms in your house, if the rooms are of approximately the same size. See the appropriate U.S. Internal Revenue Service publications for more detailed information on these and other capital improvements.

The amount of home-office expenses you deduct cannot exceed the amount of gross income you've earned from your work at home. The home-office deduction can be used to bring the taxes on what you earn at home to zero, but it can't be used as a loss to reduce taxes on the income you earn at a full-time job or from other sources. However, you can carry forward to future years the home-office expenses you were not able to deduct.

Every home-based business has expenses that are fully deductible, even if the home-office deduction is not allowed or chosen. These include:

Telephone. If you don't have a separate office line, you can deduct only the cost of long-distance calls directly related to your business. If you have a separate line, you can deduct your full expense.

Office Supplies. Deductible office supplies include envelopes, stamps, paper, pens, pencils, or any other related item.

Postage and Shipping Costs. Any expenses related to mailing, such as envelopes, stamps, and shipping material are also deductible.

Printing and Duplicating Expenses. Most businesses have printing and copying expenses, including office-generated material, manuscript copies, and duplicating expenses. All these are deductible.

Advertising and Promotion Charges. Any charges entailed in business promotion and advertising are deductible. They may include photography supplies and equipment.

Fees for Professional Service. Whenever you hire a professional to help you in your business, such as a computer repairman or accountant, the expense is deductible.

Books, Magazines, and Newspapers Related to Work. If you subscribe to newspapers, magazines, books, trade journals, or other printed material to keep you informed in your field, the expense is deductible.

Work-Related Research. Any work-related research and expenses that enable you to keep abreast of the profession and get ideas for future work are deductible.

Travel and Meals. Travel expenses related to your business, including mileage, are deductible. Deductions allowed on business meals eaten away from home keep changing, so it pays to keep up on the latest information for the current year.

Business Trips. Whenever you leave home to meet with business contacts, do work-related research at the library, buy office supplies or postage, negotiate a contract, or attend a work-related class or meeting, you are making a business trip. Even if you happen to stop at the dry cleaner or grocery store en route, the entire trip will count as business. You will, however, need to keep a log of your business and nonbusiness travel if you also use your car for trips that are just personal. The IRS allows you to deduct the cost at an ever-changing number of cents per mile, plus all parking and toll fees, so it's wise to keep up with the current amount allowed each year.

Entertainment. Home-based workers can deduct a percentage of entertainment expenses, such as restaurant meals, drinks, and tickets to such events as concerts and plays—if those expenses are used to help entertain business associates. You can also deduct expenses incurred while entertaining business associates at home, including the cost of food, drink, and flowers, and the cost of anyone you hire to help you entertain. However, this deduction keeps changing. There are strict rules for deducting business meals, such as the requirement that you have a business discussion directly preceding, directly following, or during the meal or beverage. Besides these typical entertainment expenses, business gifts are also deductible, at the current limit of up to $25 per business associate.

The IRS will not allow any expense that you can't prove with a receipt, so be sure to keep receipts. Also keep a record of people in attendance at each event, their business relationship to you, a summary of the business discussion you had, and the date. Saving a credit card receipt from a restaurant is not enough. You have to fill out the reverse side with the names of the people you entertained and a summary of the business discussion, as described, in order for the IRS to accept it as a deduction.

Business Property. Choosing whether to deduct or depreciate is the question. If your home-office furniture and equipment can be used for three years or more, you can depreciate the property. Depreciation means that you spread the deduction over the life of the equipment, rather than deducting its *entire* cost in a single tax year. You can also take furniture that was previously for personal use, put it to use in the business portion of your home, and depreciate it.

The decision to depreciate is a strategic one. If you buy expensive equipment in a year when your earnings are high, you may want to take the large deduction all at once in order to bring your taxable-income level down. If, on the other hand, you have a year when your earnings are low, you might be better off spreading out the deduction over a period of years.

OTHER TAX CONSIDERATIONS

Here are a number of other tax issues the self-employed worker needs to keep in mind:

Tax Responsibilities. When you are self-employed you don't have an employer deducting taxes from your pay throughout the year. You become responsible for making advance payments of your estimated federal income tax. Estimated tax payments are due quarterly—on April 15, June 15, September 15, and January 15. They are filed on a Form 1040–ES. At the end of the tax year, you will file a final Form 1040 with a Schedule C, which itemizes your business expenses for the whole year.

If by the end of the year you have not paid at least 90 percent of the tax you owe, or as much as you paid the year before, you may be charged substantial penalties. It's in your best interest to make your estimated tax payments during the year. This system also keeps you from owing a large sum of money all at once. If your state of residence has income taxes, as most do, you may have to make estimated tax payments throughout the year for state taxes as well.

Social Security Payments. Your estimated tax payments will also include the federal self-employment tax, Social Security. If you were employed by another person, your employer would pay half of your Social Security, and the other half would come out of your paycheck. Self-employed people must pay the full amount themselves. However, as of 1990, 50 percent of Social Security taxes are deductible.

Employment Taxes. Home-based workers who employ others must comply with many additional tax requirements. IRS Circular E, Employer's Tax Guide, covers the federal regulations, and your state tax agency can inform you of state requirements for employers.

If you employ your children or grandchildren, their earnings are deductible. Family businesses do not need to pay Social Security or unemployment taxes on minor children, and the children pay no income taxes on the first $3,000 of earned income. To substantiate this claim, keep time records of their work (the records will be more believable to the IRS if a nonrelative keeps them), note the work done, and pay family at the rate you would pay a nonfamily member for the same work.

Selling Taxable Goods and Services. With some goods and services from a home-based business, you must pay state sales tax. Taxable services differ from state to state. This is a tricky area. You may think the services you are providing are not taxable when in fact they are. It pays to check with your state tax agency to find out whether your work falls into a taxable category.

Keeping Tax Records. You need to keep complete records of your income and expenses to enable you to minimize your taxes and to help you defend yourself in the event you're audited. You must be able to substantiate any claim. Receipts are particularly crucial because they back up your claims for business expenses.

IRS PUBLICATIONS

U.S. Internal Revenue Service publications of interest for home-based workers include:

Tax Guide for Small Business, #334
Self Employment Tax, #533
Business Use of Your Home, #587
Index to Tax Publications, #900
Depreciation, #534
Tax Withholding and Declaration of Estimated Tax, #505
Tax Information for Direct Sellers, #911
Recordkeeping for a Small Business, #552
Taxpayers Starting a Business, #583

Homemade Cleaning Supplies

Sometimes you can save money by making your own cleaning supplies. Here are some "recipes":

All-purpose cleaner: In one quart of hot water, mix 1 teaspoon each of liquid soap, boric acid (borax), lemon juice, and/or vinegar. Make stronger, according to the toughness of the job, by using more of the cleaning solution in the same amount of water.

Glass cleaner: Mix 1 teaspoon vinegar or lemon juice in 1 quart water. Spray on; use newspaper to wipe dry.

Drain cleaners: To maintain clean drains, mix 1/2 cup baking soda, 1/2 cup salt, and 1/8 cup cream of tartar. Pour this mixture down drain and follow with hot water. Use this mixture immediately, since it will not remain effective if stored. Clear clogs with 1/4 cup baking soda followed by 1/2 cup vinegar. Cover drain and sink overflow vent until fizzing stops, then flush with hot water. For persistent clogs, use a plunger or metal drain snake available at hardware stores.

Oven cleaners: Clean spills as soon as the oven cools, using baking soda and hot water. Steel wool or pumice stone will remove resistant black spots. For tough stains, add salt. Do not use this method in self-cleaning or continuous-clean ovens.

Toilet bowl cleaners: Use a toilet brush and baking soda or vinegar, or use soap and borax. Remove stubborn rings with white vinegar or a pumice stone.

Mold and mildew cleaners: Make a concentrated solution of borax, vinegar, and water, then clean affected areas. Borax is an excellent inhibitor of mold growth. Keep damp areas well ventilated.

Deodorizers: To absorb odors, place baking soda or white vinegar in small dishes. Sprinkle baking soda in trash cans and kitty litter pans. House plants also absorb pollutants and purify the air.

Disinfectants: Mix 1/2 cup borax in 1 gallon hot water.

Laundry products: Soap products can be given a boost with soda and borax. Borax brightens washable fabrics and costs less than bleach. You don't always need to use the exact amount of detergent suggested on the package label. The recommended amount is based on average conditions. If your water is soft and the clothes are only lightly soiled, you can change the amount accordingly.

Metal polishes: Boil silver flatware in 2 quarts of water with 1 teaspoon baking soda, 1 teaspoon salt, and a piece of crumpled aluminum foil. Polish silver and stainless steel with a paste of baking soda and water. For brass, use equal parts of salt and flour with a little vinegar. For copper, use lemon juice or hot vinegar and salt. For chrome, use rubbing alcohol or white flour on a dry rag. For aluminum, dip cloth in lemon juice, polish, then rinse the object with warm water.

Furniture polishes: Dust furniture with a barely damp cloth. On unfinished wood, use vegetable oil to replenish luster. Polish finished wood with butcher's wax once or twice a year. Or wipe with mixture of 1 teaspoon lemon oil in 1 pint mineral or vegetable oil.

Plant sprays: Wipe leaves with mild soap and water.

Roach and ant repellent: Sprinkle powdered boric acid in cabinet edges, around baseboards, and in cracks.

Consumer Information Booklets

For the following free or inexpensive consumer information booklets write to:

R. Woods
Consumer Information Center—3A
P.O. Box 100
Pueblo, Colorado 81002

MONEY MANAGEMENT

Financial Tools Used in Money Management. How to use savings, investments, insurance and credit to best achieve your financial goals.—22 pp. (1987, USD), 127Z, $1.50.

Financial Institutions: Consumer Rights. How and where to complain if you have a problem with a bank, savings and loan association, or credit union.—(1990, FFIEC) 442Z, 50 cents.

Consumer Credit Handbook. How to apply for credit, what to do if it's denied, and how to correct mistakes on your credit report.—46 pp. (1986, FRB), 439Z, 50 cents.

Choosing and Using Credit Cards. Credit cards vary widely in their charges and how fees are calculated. Learn how to compare rates for the best deal.—5 pp. (1991, FTC), 438Z, 50 cents.

A Consumer's Guide to Life Insurance. Life insurance is to provide future financial security for your family. Here's a guide to different types of policies, costs, and coverage. Includes a glossary.—30 pp., revised edition (1992, USDA), 440Z, 50 cents.

Fair Credit Reporting Act. How to check the data in your credit report and what to do if it's incorrect.—7 pp. (1987, FDIC), 441Z, 50 cents.

Looking Out for #2: A Married Couple's Guide to Understanding Your Benefit Choices at Retirement. *Defined Benefit Plan* . . . pays a fixed benefit at retirement.—38 pp. (1991, IRS), 443Z, 50 cents.

Defined Contribution Plan . . . is determined by you and your employer's contribution.—42 pp. (1991, IRS), 444Z, 50 cents.

Solving Credit Problems. Explains why your credit history is important, and how to establish a good one. Helpful tips on dealing with credit and debt problems and where to find low-cost help.—4 pp. (1992, FTC), 445Z, 50 cents.

Staying Independent: Planning for Financial Independence in Later Life. Helps you evaluate your present financial status and determine if changes are necessary.—7 pp. (1990, USDA), 446Z, 50 cents.

Building Your Future with Annuities. An annuity is tax-deferred money, set aside for future use, typically at retirement. Discusses various types, features, costs, what to look for, and more.—13 pp. (1992, USDA), 571Z, Free.

Facts about Financial Planners. Discusses what financial planners can and can't do, how to evaluate credentials, what to expect regarding costs, and more.—13 pp. (1990, FTC), 447Z, 50 cents.

Information about Marketable Treasury Securities. Learn about bills, notes, and bonds sold through your local Federal Reserve Bank or Bureau of the Public Debt.—16 pp. (1992, TREA), 572Z, Free.

Investment Swindles: How They Work and How to Avoid Them. How to protect yourself against illegal, legitimate-sounding telemarketing and direct mail offers.—20 pp. (1987, CFTC), 573Z, Free.

Investor's Bill of Rights. Tips to help you make an informed decision when purchasing investments.—7 pp. (1987, CFTC/USPS), 574Z, Free.

Money Matters. Tips for selecting the best financial planner, tax preparer, real estate broker, or lawyer. How to get the help you want at the price you've agreed on.—13 pp. (1986, FTC), 448Z, 50 cents.

The Savings Bonds Question and Answer Book. Detailed information on savings bonds, including purchase, interest, maturity, replacement, redemption, exchange, and taxes.—12 pp. (1991, TREA), 449Z, 50 cents.

Understanding Opportunities and Risks in Futures Trading. Explains the commodities market, including the risks involved and regulations governing it.—46 pp. (1986, CFTC), 451Z, 50 cents.

FOOD

Thrifty Meals for Two. A guide on how to shop for and prepare hearty, nutritious, and economical meals. Includes menus and recipes.—69 pp. (1985, USDA), 118Z, $2.50.

Eating for Life. Tips on making healthy food choices that may reduce your risk of developing cancer and heart disease.—23 pp. (1992, NIH), 115Z, $1.00.

Eating to Lower Your High Blood Cholesterol. Here is a guide to help you choose, go easy on, and decrease certain foods. Includes menus, guidelines, cooking tips, and comparison charts to help teach you how to eat healthily.—53 pp. (1987, NIH), 116Z, $2.00.

Food Guide Pyramid. Your daily diet should look like a pyramid—a lot of breads and cereals at the base, and only a few fats, oils, and sweets at the top. Here's how to use this concept to eat right and maintain a healthy weight.—30 pp. (1992, USDA), 117Z, $1.00.

Quick Consumer Guide to Safe Food Handling. To avoid food poisoning, learn how long some foods can be safely frozen or refrigerated.—8 pp. (1990, USDA), 528Z, Free.

HEALTH CARE

Facing Forward: A Guide for Cancer Survivors. Advice on coping with the psychological, physical, and financial effects of this illness. Practical information on health care, insurance coverage, job concerns, and more.—45 pp. (1990, NIH), 531Z, Free.

An FDA Guide to Dieting. New research on how genetics, the kind of calories you eat, your metabolism, and the exercise you get all affect weight.—4 pp. (1991, FDA), 512Z, Free.

Rx to OTC. What you need to know about prescription medications that have become available over the counter.—3 pp. (1992, FDA), 546Z, Free.

Getting a Second Opinion. Answers questions you might have and includes a toll-free number for locating specialists.—5 pp. (1989, HCFA), 550Z, Free.

So You Have High Blood Cholesterol. Practical guidelines for lowering your blood cholesterol through diet, medication, and exercise.—28 pp. (1987, NIH), 122Z, $1.00.

Depression. Nine million people suffer from depressive illness during any six-month period. Learn its symptoms and causes, how it's diagnosed and treated, and how to help.—4 pp. (1989, NIMH), 557Z, Free.

What to Do When a Friend Is Depressed. Identifies common myths and warning signals, and suggests ways to help.—6 pp. (1989, NIMH), 564Z, Free.

Mutual Help Groups. Gain strength through sharing with others who have similar problems; an overview of the many support groups available.—6 pp. (1989, NIMH), 558Z, Free.

Stress. Suggestions to help effectively deal with stress.—1 p. (1987, NIMH), 563Z, Free.

You Are Not Alone. Learn the facts about mental health and illness so you can get help for yourself or a loved one. Describes behavior that may indicate a problem and how to find help.—9 pp. (1985, NIMH), 566Z, Free.

A Consumer's Guide to Mental Health Services. Answers commonly asked questions, helps identify warning signals, discusses various treatments, and lists resources for help and information.—28 pp. (1987, NIMH), 556Z, Free.

Seal Out Dental Decay. Describes how dental sealants can prevent tooth decay in young children.—6 pp. (1991, NIH), 418Z, 50 cents.

Calories and Weight. Calorie tables for hundreds of popular foods and beverages.—114 pp. (1990, USDA), 107Z, $1.75.

Getting Fit Your Way. A 12-week program to help make exercise a lifelong habit with an emphasis on strengthening your heart, quitting smoking, and losing weight.—47 pp. (1989, DOD), 108Z, $3.75.

Walking for Exercise and Pleasure. Includes illustrated warm-up exercise and advice on how far, how fast, and how often to walk for best results.—14 pp. (1986, PCPFS), 109Z, $1.00.

Guide to Health Insurance for People with Medicare. Fill in gaps in Medicare coverage and avoid paying for duplicate benefits.—14 pp. (1992, HCFA), 515Z, Free.

The Medicare Handbook. Learn who is eligible, how to apply, how to fill out claims, what is and isn't covered, and your right to appeal.—41 pp. (1992, HCFA), 111Z, $3.00.

Medicare Q & A. Answers 60 commonly asked questions about Medicare—eligibility, enrollment, who pays deductibles, services, benefits, and much more.—16 pp. (1991, HCFA), 517Z, Free.

Health Benefits under COBRA (Consolidated Omnibus Budget Reconciliation Act). Helps you keep or buy coverage for yourself and family after a job loss, reduced work hours, divorce, or death.—18 pp. (1990, DOL), 509Z, Free.

Funerals: A Consumer Guide. Lists the information about fees, goods, and services that a funeral provider is required to give you, whether you inquire in person or by phone.—4 pp., revised edition (1992, FTC), 459Z, 50 cents.

TRAVEL

Discover America: A Listing of State and Territorial Travel Offices of the United States. Use this list to order free vacation information, including maps, calendars of events, travel guides, and more.—8 pp. (1990, DOI), 455Z, 50 cents.

A Guide to Your National Forests. A map showing each national forest and information offices to help you plan your visit.—(1989, USDA), 133Z, $1.00.

The National Wildlife Refuges. Fold-out map listing the facilities and best viewing seasons at over 300 wildlife refuges nationwide.—(1991 DOI), 137Z, $1.00.

STUDENTS

The Student Guide: Financial Aid. Describes federal grants, loans, and work-study programs for college, vocational, and technical school students.—58 pp. (1992–1993, ED), 520Z, Free.

School Shopping Tips. If you need more education for a better job, here are resources and some helpful information about choosing a career, finding the right vocational school, and getting financial aid.—15 pp. (1992, ED), 511Z, Free.

U.S. Savings Bonds for Education. Here are questions and answers that highlight the new educational benefit of Series EE Savings Bonds.—7 pp. (1992, TREA), 450Z, 50 cents.

TRANSPORTATION

Auto Service Contracts. Helpful tips on avoiding duplicate coverage, checking out the service provider, making claims, using reconditioned parts, and much more.—4 pp. (1991, FTC), 402Z, 50 cents.

Consumer Tire Guide. Learn how to check for proper air pressure and signs of uneven wear, how and who to rotate your tires, special care in cold weather, and more.—12 pp. (1990, DOT), 403Z, 50 cents.

Cost of Owning and Operating Automobiles, Vans and Light Trucks. Discusses depreciation, maintenance, gas, insurance, taxes, and much more, based on 1991 prices.—28 pp. (DOT), 404Z, 50 cents.

Gas Mileage Guides. Lists miles per gallon estimates for city and highway driving. Gas Mileage Guide: 1993.—16 pp. (1992, DOE/EPA), 501Z, Free.

New Car Buying Guide. Discusses pricing terms, financing options, and various contracts. Includes a worksheet to help you bargain.—3 pp. (1988, FTC), 405Z, 50 cents.

Nine Ways to Lower Your Auto Insurance Costs. Tips on what to do to lower your expenses. Includes a chart to compare discounts and a list of state insurance departments.—6 pp. (1990, OCA), 406Z, 50 cents.

Recycling Used Oil. Gives easy-to-follow directions for changing your oil. Explains how and why oil recycling helps the environment and saves energy.—3 pp. (1991, EPA), 503Z, Free.

What You Should Know about Your Auto Emissions Warranty. If your car fails an emissions test, you may be entitled to free repairs. Learn how to make a claim, what parts and repairs are covered, and more.—8 pp. (1988, EPA), 407Z, 50 cents.

TAXES

Your Federal Income Tax. IRS Publication No.17. You can get the free guide by calling 1–800–829–3676.

Tax Counseling for the Elderly. Trained volunteers and IRS staffers provide free income-tax consultations and return preparations for those who are 60 and older. For information, call 1–800–829–1040.

HOME BUSINESS

Financial Management: How to Make a Go of Your Business. Here's an overview of financial and management essentials for a better chance at success.—71 pp. (1986, SBA), 128Z, $2.50.

General Information Concerning Patents. Learn what can be patented, how to apply, costs, and more on patent law and procedures. Includes application.—48 pp., revised edition (1992, FRB), 452Z, 50 cents.

Reporting and Disclosure Guide for Employee Benefits Plans. Useful for a small business considering employee pension and welfare plans. Charts various federal reporting forms and gives filing dates.—1 p. (1991, DOL), 576Z, Free.

Starting and Managing a Business from Your Home. Help with assessing your skills, experience, and goals, evaluating your product and market, financial planning, zoning insurance, and more.—54 pp. (1988, SBA), 130Z, $1.75.

The Small Business Directory. Lists booklets and videotapes to help start and manage a successful small business.—12 pp. (1992, SBA), 577Z, Free.

Veteran's Handbook. Highlights SBA programs for veterans interested in starting, financing, and managing a small business.—5 pp. (1988, SBA), 453Z, 50 cents.

HOUSING

Consumer Handbook on Adjustable Rate Mortgages. Basic features, advantages, risks, and terminology associated with adjustable rate mortgages.—25 pp. (1984, FRB), 423Z, 50 cents.

Home Buyer's Vocabulary. Defines common words and terms used in the real estate world. Especially useful for the first-time buyer.—14 pp. (1987, HUD), 123Z, $1.00.

A Home of Your Own. Advice on choosing and buying a home. Answers questions about buying FHA insured homes that have been foreclosed and reverted to HUD ownership.—30 pp. (1990, HUD), 568Z, Free.

Reverse Mortgages. How to convert home equity into cash— explains the three types of reverse mortgages available and how to get information on home equity conversion plans.—3 pp. (1991, FTC), 427Z, 50 cents.

When Your Home Is on the Line. Your home serves as collateral for a home equity loan. Here are questions, terms, tips, a checklist, and more—all to help you find the best deal.—16 pp. (1989, FRB), 428Z, 50 cents.

Wise Home Buying. Here's help in finding the right house: when to use a broker, when to get an inspection, and shopping for a mortgage.—24 pp. (1987, HUD), 124Z, $1.00.

OTHER PUBLICATIONS

Protecting Your Privacy. How to check your credit file and medical record, handle telephone sales, and have your name removed from mailing lists.—5 pp. (1990, OCA), 590Z, Free.

Consumer's Resource Handbook. Lists contacts to help with consumer questions or complaints. Includes corporate consumer representatives, private resolution programs, automobile manufacturers, federal, state, and local government agencies with consumer responsibilities, how to write an effective complaint letter, and much more.—96 pp. (1992, OCA), 592Z, Free.

INDEX

Vacations, 75
Volunteer work, 118–19

Wedding consultant, 117
Wellness plan, 64. *See also* Health
 care
Widow, lesson from, 42
Wills, 145

Woodworking, 117
Word processing service, 117
Work: joy of, 102–3; unpaid, 103–5;
 home-based, 105–18; volunteer,
 118–19; meaningful, 119–20;
 blessings from, 121
Writing services, 106–10, 116–17